EXPLORING

MARTHA'S VINEYARD

BY BIKE, FOOT, AND KAYAK

SECOND EDITION

Exploring

MARTHA'S VINEYARD

BY BIKE, FOOT, AND KAYAK

SECOND EDITION

LEE SINAI

Illustrated by
JOYCE S. SHERR

APPALACHIAN MOUNTAIN CLUB BOOKS
BOSTON, MASSACHUSETTS

Cover Photographs: Alison Shaw
All photographs by the authors unless otherwise noted
Book Design: Stephanie Doyle
Map Design: Carol Bast Tyler
Illustrations: Joyce S. Sherr

Library of Congress Cataloging-in-Publication Data

The paper used in this publication meets the minimum requirements
of the American National Standard for Information Sciences—
Permanence of Paper for Printed Library Materials, ANSI
Z39.48–1984.∞

**Due to changes in conditions,
use of the information in this book
is at the sole risk of the user.**

Printed on recycled paper using soy-based inks.
Printed in the United States of America.

10 9 8 7 6 5 4 3 2   01 02 03

CONTENTS

OFF-ROAD BIKING

WALKING AND HIKING

Edgartown

Chappaquiddick

Oak Bluffs

West Tisbury

Chilmark

KAYAKING

ACKNOWLEDGMENTS

I am grateful to many people for their gracious contributions to this book. My family, especially, deserves heartfelt thanks. Allen, Lauren, and Todd were encouraging and tremendously helpful in the editing and design of this book.

I am most appreciative of the time and information accorded me by James Lengyell, director, and Adam Moore, land superintendent, of the Martha's Vineyard Land Bank; Dick Johnson, director of the Sheriff's Meadow Foundation; John Varkonda, superintendent of the Manuel F. Corellus State Forest; and Tom Chase, naturalist for the Trustees of Reservations.

Charles Clifford, director of the Martha's Vineyard Commission, graciously allowed me to use the commission's maps, and Jan Paul hunted them down and sent them to me.

Chris Kennedy, director of the Trustees of Reservations, also kindly shared information and maps, as did Alice Mohrman and Rebecca Taylor, naturalists at the Felix Neck Wildlife Sanctuary.

Professor George Ellmore of Tufts University willingly shared his botanical expertise. Carol Knapp was most helpful in the identification of wildflowers and grasses.

I am most grateful to my friends who read and commented on chapters, tested the bike rides and hikes, and were always supportive. Special thanks to Melissa Norton and Jin Park, my computer gurus, along with Susan Sewall, Rhoda Fischer, Arlene Deardorff, Chris Miller, and Jack and Norma Arnow for their help. Joyce Sherr, the illustrator, also provided information and helpful advice.

INTRODUCTION

Welcome to Martha's Vineyard, a popular island that has managed to retain its unique appeal. One reason for the Vineyard's popularity and a key to its allure is its large number of unspoiled scenic areas. Farsighted philanthropists and aggressive land conservation have allowed the Vineyard to remain as it was centuries ago. Once you step off the ferry or airplane and leave the town centers, you feel as if you truly have escaped from the mainland. Tranquil sanctuaries, picturesque ponds, and miles of bike paths encourage a "get-away-from-it-all" experience. Discovering these often obscure spots can be a real challenge. In this book I tell you how to find these places and then guide you through them on bike, foot, and kayak while pointing out their history and unique natural features. *Exploring Martha's Vineyard by Bike, Foot, and Kayak* serves as a comprehensive guide to the Vineyard, since it describes the island's major attractions as well as its hidden treasures.

For an island with six decidedly different towns and a wide variety of natural resources, Martha's Vineyard is surprisingly compact, stretching just twenty-three miles from the Aquinnah cliffs at its western end to the Chappaquiddick beaches at its eastern end. Because the island is small and has fairly level terrain, it's an ideal place to bike and hike. With recent additions, the island now boasts thirty-five miles of bike paths which allow for a relaxing exploration, without worries about traffic, parking, or speed limits.

Martha's Vineyard is famous for miles of gorgeous coastline and sandy beaches, but its other less-well-known but equally picturesque assets are its large ponds and bays, often rimmed by long, thin coves. The best way to explore these bodies of water is by canoe or kayak. Paddling encourages a leisurely exploration of inlets and coves and allows the flexibility to stop and swim at remote beaches or hike on conservation land. In this book you'll discover twelve bodies of water that permit public access and have designated spots for unloading your water craft and parking your car.

Exploring Martha's Vineyard by Bike, Foot, and Kayak contains forty-four chapters. The first fourteen describe rides for bicyclists, eight that tour the island on paved roads and six that go off-road to explore footpaths, bridle trails, and old carriage lanes. The next eighteen chapters acquaint you with the places you can explore on foot, including beaches, towns, wildlife preserves, and conservation areas. The fourth section of the book, Kayaking, contains the best areas for kayaking and canoeing. Each chapter directs you to a pond and alerts you to special places to pull up your boat and explore or swim.

Each of the On-Road Biking chapters originates from one of the three most populous towns: Edgartown, Vineyard Haven, and Oak Bluffs. I have included directions from the other two towns so cyclists can pedal the route from any of these three starting points. These chapters contain maps with detailed explanations of the routes, interesting sights along the way, locations of public restrooms, and places to buy food and drink.

The Off-Road chapters include a sample of off-road riding from most towns. Many of the routes in the Walking and Hiking chapters are also suitable for biking. Check the chart to locate these areas.

The bike rides vary in length and difficulty in order to appeal to both adults and children of all abilities. Don't let the distances intimidate you. Since most of the roads are flat, it's easy to cover twenty miles in two hours. You'll have many opportunities to catch your breath during the frequent stops that are built into the trips. Do allow enough time for your explorations so you can leisurely investigate whatever is of interest.

Both the Hiking and Walking as well as the Kayaking sections include maps and specific directions, and describe the geological, botanical, and historical features of each area.

THE CHART

The chart at the front of this guide (p. xxvi) allows you to find quickly the biking and walking explorations that best suit your preferences. It lists routes for school-age children and also indicates where swimming and dogs are allowed. A quick check will reveal the length and level of difficulty of each exploration, and if there is an entry fee.

HOW TO USE THIS BOOK

Before you start out on one of the explorations, read through the entire chapter and look over the maps, which have been designed to use in conjunction with the written directions. The directions are numbered to help guide you through each outing. Each successive number indicates a change in direction. If faced with a situation where there is no number change or directions, continue straight on the main path or road. In the biking chapters additional information—historical, botanical, and/or geological—is indented below the direction. This format gives you the choice of reading the information or skipping over it to focus only on the directions. Most of the bike rides and walks form loops, in order to cover different terrain on your return.

Your bicycle model will make some destinations more or less accessible. Unless you own or can rent a mountain or hybrid bike, you will find riding on unpaved roads quite challenging. A mountain or hybrid bike will give you greater traction on the sometimes sandy bike paths, better maneuverability on primitive roads, and the option of biking off-road. If you have a touring bike and are determined to reach a specific destination, you can walk your bike on these sandy or rocky sections. Each chapter and the chart (on page xxvi) indicate what type of terrain to expect and which properties permit biking on their trails.

Since walking allows for a more leisurely examination of the habitat than biking, the Walks and Hikes chapters contain more botanical information. In these chapters you will find words in **boldface type** that point out a noteworthy site, tree, bush, flower, or fowl and often have accompanying drawings for help in identification.

Although each chapter has been pretested, words and directions can be misinterpreted and intersection markers may be missing. If you lose your way, don't worry; rediscovering the route is part of the adventure.

In order to preserve what nature has kindly bestowed, please stay on marked trails, leave nothing behind, and take out only what you bring in.

TERMINOLOGY

T intersection: The road on which you are traveling ends, requiring a right or left turn onto the intersected road. This junction forms a T.

Bear or bend left or right: Turn at a wide angle (about 120°).

Merge: The road or trail joins another road.

USEFUL GEAR

Before setting out on your exploration, make sure you have the necessary gear. Also check your bike carefully to prevent being stranded because of faulty brakes or a flat tire. In the appendix at the end of this book you'll find a list of emergency phone numbers and addresses. Also included are phone numbers of bicycle shops and service stations should your tires need air.

THE FOLLOWING IS A CHECKLIST OF USEFUL ITEMS:

Insect repellent
Water
Sunscreen
Sunglasses
Tissues
Money
High-energy snacks
Bandanna or small hand towel
Small first-aid kit
Windbreaker
Towel, if swimming destination
Long pants, if wooded destination

Optional but useful equipment for cyclists
Bike lock
Tool kit
Odometer
Handlebar bag with transparent map holder

Mountain Biking

In order to preserve the areas open to mountain bikers, please follow these rules:

1. Keep off trails posted with No Biking signs.
2. Stay on the trails. Never create new ones.
3. Do not ride between January 1 and April 30.
4. Practice low-impact cycling: Dismount in areas where your tires will leave an imprint, such as wetlands, moist stream beds, or on certain soils after a heavy rain; avoid skidding when ascending or descending steep slopes.
5. Always relinquish the right of way to other trail users.
6. When meeting horseback riders, dismount until the horse has passed.
7. Ride in control.
8. Alert other trail users if you intend to pass.
9. Don't ride alone.

Safety

Martha's Vineyard is a terrific place for cyclists. The bike paths will protect you from most road hazards. However, even on bike paths there are dangers:

1. Driveways and side roads that intersect the bike path. Drivers do not always notice cyclists on bike paths. Always slow down and check to see if a vehicle is approaching; if one is, **assume that it will not give you the right of way.** Make eye contact with the driver before passing in front of his vehicle.
2. Pedestrians. Joggers and walkers also use bike paths. Pedestrians usually yield if you say, "Excuse me," followed by, "On your left," or, "On your right," depending on which side you will be passing. When passing, be sure to look ahead for traffic coming from the opposite direction.
3. Other cyclists. Many riders ride two or three abreast on the path. Others stop in the middle. Again, a polite, "Excuse me," followed by your passing direction should suffice.
4. Sand and gravel. Sand is everywhere. Watch out for skidding when turning or braking.

While on bike paths, follow the rules of the road. Ride single file on the right-hand side. If you have to stop, pull over to one side so you will not obstruct traffic.

Not every Vineyard road has a bike path, so often you will have to share the road with cars, trucks, motorcycles, and mopeds. Although the routing in this book protects you from riding on the busiest and most dangerous roads, you will encounter traffic, particularly during July and August. Your best protection is to be alert, defensive, and cautious. Hug the side of the road. Use hand signals. Ride single file.

POISON IVY AND TICKS

Even a spot as wonderful as the Vineyard presents potential problems. Poison ivy and ticks exist on the island but should not bother you if you take the proper precautions. To avoid **poison ivy,** which grows all over the island, you have to know what it looks like—clusters of three green leaves, which are shiny if the plant grows in a sunny spot and dull if it is in the shade. In autumn its leaves turn bright red and it sprouts white berries. The ivy can grow like a vine, circling a tree trunk, or it can spread

Poison ivy

along the ground among bushes or on sand dunes. If your skin comes into contact with poison ivy, wash the affected areas with strong soap as soon as possible.

Dog tick

Deer tick

Ticks live on tall beach grass and in brushy areas. You often can see them hanging on to the tips of grasses or leaves waiting to grab on to a warm-blooded traveler. These arachnids come in two varieties, the pinhead-size deer tick and the quarter-inch dog tick. They usually attach to legs and then move upward. It takes them from four to forty-eight hours to break through the skin. If left undetected, the tick can swell to an inch in size and is capable of transmitting a number of diseases. Lyme disease, carried by the deer tick, is the one that people fear most.

To prevent a tick from attaching to your skin, wear long pants tucked into high socks when walking or pedaling through tall grass or bushy areas. Avoid hiking through any untracked patches of brush. Walk in the middle of trails and avoid brushing against foliage. Use high-strength DEET repellent on your clothing. Wear light-colored clothes, so you can see if any ticks are on you. They are easy to remove if they haven't attached. Always examine yourself thoroughly when you return home, especially the scalp, legs, and underarms. If you find a tick on you, do not panic. Most ticks do not carry disease. Pull off the tick by grasping its head and pulling upward. Dispose of the tick by immersing it in alcohol or soapy water, and then wash your hands thoroughly. If you develop a skin rash around the bite and/or flulike symptoms, see a doctor and tell him about the tick bite. Antibiotics are effective in the early treatment of Lyme disease.

KAYAKING

Paddling around the numerous ponds, coves, and bays on Martha's Vineyard can be a relaxing way to explore the island. A few precautions are in order: Be mindful of the wind and tides—listen to the weather forecasts and check the tide charts, which appear weekly in Vineyard newspapers. A potentially relaxing paddle can turn into a stressful struggle if you have to battle current and wind. Usually the best time to paddle is in the morning. During July and August southwest winds often increase in the midafternoon. When possible, I have tried to design the routes so the wind is at your back on the return.

Wear shoes to protect your feet from sharp shells and a brimmed hat to save your head, face, and neck from the sun, which is doubly dangerous when reflected off the water. Slather on sun lotion, take plenty of water, and don't forget a life vest.

GETTING TO THE VINEYARD

If you are arriving on Martha's Vineyard by ferry, you can bring your bicycle with you for a modest extra charge. Ferries to Martha's Vineyard leave from New Bedford, Hyannis, Falmouth, and Woods Hole, Massachusetts.

The Schamonchi (508-997-1688) out of New Bedford takes ninety minutes and makes four roundtrips daily in the summer. The Hy-Line (508-775-7185) from Hyannis also makes four ninety-minute runs each day. The Island Queen (508-548-4800) leaves from Falmouth more frequently, is less expensive, and takes only thirty-five minutes. These ferries run only from Memorial Day to Columbus Day, disembark in Oak Bluffs, and do not carry cars.

The Falmouth Ferry Service runs from Falmouth to Edgartown and takes one hour. It runs six times a day in the summer and four times a day in spring and fall (508-548-9400).

The Woods Hole, Martha's Vineyard, and Nantucket Steamship Authority boats are larger, carry cars, and run year-round. The trip takes forty-five minutes and lands in either Vineyard Haven or Oak Bluffs. However, parking in Woods Hole can be a problem. In Falmouth there is a parking lot next to the Island Queen. In Woods Hole passengers must ride a shuttle bus or bike from the parking lot to the ferry dock. The 3.25-mile Shining Sea Bikeway, located 0.25 mile to the right of Palmer Street Parking, leads to the Steamship Authority dock in Woods Hole.

If you arrive on the Vineyard by plane, you can hail a cab or ride a shuttle bus to your lodgings and rent a bike at one of the bike rental shops listed in the appendix.

ISLAND FACILITIES

To support the Vineyarders' constant crusade to reduce the number of automobiles, the Martha's Vineyard Transit Authority runs a popular island-wide bus system that operates from Memorial Day to mid-September. Some buses are equipped with bike racks. Pick up a schedule when you arrive.

The Martha's Vineyard Family Campground (508-693-3772), open from mid-May to mid-October, is situated 0.5 mile from Vineyard Haven Center on the Edgartown–Vineyard Haven Road.

Hostelling International (508-693-2665), open from April 1 to November 6, abuts the Manuel Correllus State Forest in West Tisbury.

Up-Island, Down-Island, Wet and Dry

Visitors are often confused by island terminology. If a place is referred to as "down-island," the location is the eastern end of the island in the towns of Edgartown, Vineyard Haven, or Oak Bluffs. Of those towns, Edgartown and Oak Bluffs are "wet," which means their restaurants are permitted to serve liquor. If you go to dinner up-island, to Chilmark, West Tisbury, or Aquinnah, bring your own wine or beer because these towns are dry.

THE HISTORY OF
MARTHA'S VINEYARD

Martha's Vineyard, the largest island in New England, was formed from glacial melt after the last period of glaciation. In North America the center of the glacier was near Hudson Bay, where ice piled up to 10,000 feet. The pressure from its weight forced the ice to flow westward and southward. It spread over most of North America, as far south as the latitude of Martha's Vineyard. When the ice began to melt about fifteen thousand years ago, all the loose rocks, soil, and gravel the ice sheet had picked up as it inched along were left behind. At the ice sheet's final stopping place, called the terminal moraine, millions of tons of rocks, sand, and other debris poured off the glacier, accumulating enough mass to form Martha's Vineyard and Cape Cod.

During this Pleistocene epoch much of the earth's water was frozen into glaciers. As the ice melted, the level of the sea rose by as much as 100 feet. Martha's Vineyard became separated from Cape Cod more than fifteen thousand years ago, when the sea rose high enough to cover low-lying land areas such as Nantucket Sound, Vineyard Sound, and Buzzards Bay.

Archaeological evidence indicates that the island's earliest inhabitants were Native Americans who lived here as early as five thousand years ago. When the English arrived they referred to the indigenous people as the Wampanoags, meaning "easterners." The names of towns, ponds, and rivers such as Chappaquiddick, Sengekontacket, Mattakeeset, and Menemsha, are constant reminders of these early settlers. Today, many of the island's remaining Wampanoags live in Aquinnah (Gay Head).

Martha's Vineyard was named for the daughter of Captain Bartholomew Gosnold, who landed in the Cape Poge area of Chappaquidick in 1602. Gosnold added the word "vineyard" because of the "incredible store of [grape] vines," which grew all over the island.

In 1641, for the grand sum of forty pounds, Thomas Mayhew of Watertown, Massachusetts, purchased Martha's Vineyard, Nantucket, and the Elizabeth Islands from two English noblemen. His son, Thomas Jr., along with other Englishmen, came to the Vineyard soon after the purchase and settled in Great Harbor, now named Edgartown.

These early English settlers, consisting of about eighty people, learned fishing, farming, and whaling from the friendly Wampanoags. The English in turn shared their Christian beliefs, particularly Reverend Thomas Mayhew Jr., who successfully converted many Wampanoags to Christianity. When the Reverend did not return from a transatlantic voyage, his father, governor of the island, continued his son's missionary work. Three succeeding generations of Mayhews also were influential island preachers.

The sea and land provided sustenance for the English as it had for the Native Americans. As the number of settlers increased, they scattered all over the island. Six distinct Vineyard towns grew and each developed its own character based on how its occupants earned a living. Even today, each town has maintained an individuality that reflects its origins.

Vineyard Haven, which is incorporated as the town of Tisbury, was a popular port for the vessels that sold the Vineyard's whale oil, candles, salt cod, and wool to customers in Europe and all down the American coast to the West Indies. Its residents earned their living from the sea as sailors, pilots, navigators, and fishermen. Today Vineyard Haven's well-located harbor continues to be the island's main port of entry, welcoming the Martha's Vineyard Steamship Authority ferry year-round. As a result, it is the only town in which stores and restaurants remain open during the winter.

Oak Bluffs owes its origins to the resurgence of religion that sparked the annual summer gatherings at the Martha's Vineyard Camp Meeting Grounds. The festive nature of these meetings created a resortlike atmosphere which pervaded all aspects of Oak Bluffs' development—from the ornate and colorful gingerbread cottages to the tourist-friendly shops.

The development of **Edgartown** was heavily influenced by the lucrative whaling industry. Homes, churches, and public buildings were built with whaling profits. The community today reflects the wealth of the captains and businessmen who lived there two hundred years ago.

Although physically separated from Edgartown, the island of **Chappaquiddick** is governed by Edgartown. "Chappy's" inaccessibility prevented the English from moving there until the middle of the nineteenth century. Chappaquiddick remains relatively rural, with only one major road and one store. Its residents prefer the sense of isolation that comes from living on an island distinct from the parent island. Its beaches, although magnificent, are difficult to reach, since they lie at the end of quite primitive roads.

The residents of centrally located **West Tisbury** had no port and were forced to rely on farming to support their families. The town continues to resemble a typical New England farming community, with its general store and old Agricultural Hall, which houses a weekly farmers' market. During the third week of August the new Agricultural Hall is the site of one of the island's most popular events: the Martha's Vineyard Agricultural Society Fair and Livestock Show.

Chilmark resembles a town in Vermont, with its rolling hills, winding roads, and tall, leafy trees. The town maintains its rural character by requiring that each home have at least three acres of land. Chilmark's early settlers derived their living from the sea, a tradition that continues in the fishing village of Menemsha. Its picturesque harbor holds many draggers that fish the local waters.

Aquinnah, formerly known as Gay Head, began as an Native American settlement and continues to be one of the two Indian townships in Massachusetts. The town is famous for its multicolored cliffs, whose sediments reveal deposits and fossils millions of years old.

LOCATOR MAP

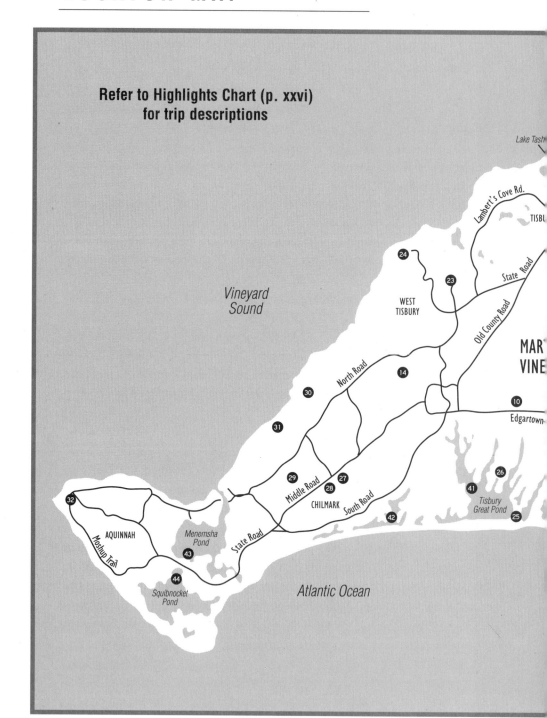

**Refer to Highlights Chart (p. xxvi)
for trip descriptions**

Lake Tash

Lambert's Cove Rd.

TISBU

State Road

Vineyard
Sound

WEST
TISBURY

Old County Road

MAR
VINE

24

23

North Road

14

30

10

Edgartown

31

26

29

Middle Road

27

41

Tisbury
Great Pond

32

28

CHILMARK

South Road

25

AQUINNAH

Menemsha
Pond

42

Moshup Trail

State Road

43

44

Squibnocket
Pond

Atlantic Ocean

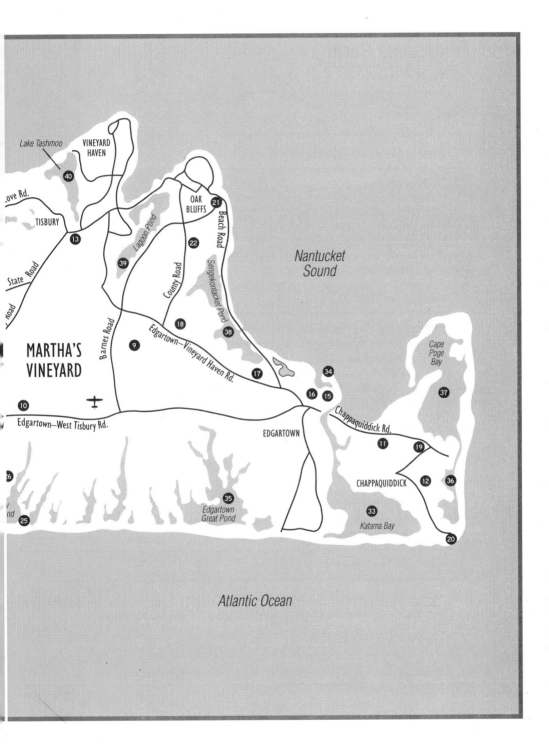

Lake Tashmoo

VINEYARD
HAVEN

ove Rd.

40

TISBURY

State Road

13

OAK
BLUFFS

21

Beach Road

Lagoon Pond

22

39

County Road

Sengekontacket Pond

Nantucket
Sound

MARTHA'S
VINEYARD

18

9

Barnes Road

Edgartown–Vineyard Haven Rd.

38

17

34

16 15

Cape
Poge
Bay

37

10

Edgartown–West Tisbury Rd.

Chappaquiddick Rd.

EDGARTOWN

11

19

CHAPPAQUIDDICK

12

36

26

25

35

Edgartown
Great Pond

33

Katama Bay

20

Atlantic Ocean

HIGHLIGHTS CHART

BIKING	Miles	Difficulty*	Off-Road Biking Permitted
1. Vineyard Haven/Oak Bluffs/Edgartown Loop	16.4	E	✔
2. Chappaquiddick	12.8	E	✔
3. Katama Point/South Beach Loop	23	E	
4. Vineyard Haven/West Chop/Herring Creek	17–20	E	
5. West Tisbury South Loop	25	E	✔
6. West Tisbury North Loop	13–19	M	✔
7. Chilmark Loop	34	M	✔
8. Aquinnah and Lobsterville Loop	42–46	H	
9. Manuel F. Correllus State Forest/East	6	E	✔
Connector	2	E	✔
10. Manuel F. Correllus State Forest/West	5	M	✔
11. Brine's Pond/Chappy Five Corners	3	E	✔
12. Poucha Pond Reservation	1.8	E	✔
13. Tisbury Meadow/Wompesket/Ripley's Field	6	M	✔
14. Waskosim's Rock Reservation	4.5	M	✔

*Difficulty: E=Easy, M=Moderate, S=Strenuous

Suitable for Children	Dogs Allowed	Fees	Swimming	Primitive Access Roads	Historical Interest
✔			✔		
✔		✔	✔	✔	
✔			✔		
		✔	✔	✔	✔
			✔		
			✔	✔	✔
			✔		
			✔		
✔	✔				
✔	✔				
	✔				
✔	✔				
✔	✔				
	✔				
	✔				

Highlights Chart

Walking and Hiking	Miles	Difficulty*	Off-Road Biking Permitted
15. Edgartown—Lighthouse Beach	3.4	E	
16. Sheriff's Meadow Sanctuary	0.5	E	
17. Caroline Tuthill Wildlife Preserve	1.4	E	
18. Felix Neck Wildlife Sanctuary	2	E	
19. Mytoi—Dike Bridge—East Beach	1	E	
20. Wasque Reservation	3	E	✔
21. Camp Meeting Grounds	1.3	E	
22. Trade Wind Fields Preserve	1.3–3	E	✔
23. Christiantown—Christiantown Woods	0.5	E	✔
24. Cedar Tree Neck Wildlife Sanctuary	2.8	M	
25. Long Point Wildlife Refuge	3	E	✔
26. Sepiessa Point Reservation	2.5	E	✔
27. Middle Road Sanctuary	2.7	M	
28. Fulling Mill Brook Preserve	2.3	E/M	✔
29. Peaked Hill Reservation	1.5	M	✔
30. Great Rock Bight Preserve	1.5	E/M	✔
31. Menemsha Hills Reservation	3	M	
32. Aquinnah Cliffs—Aquinnah Beach	1+	E	

*Difficulty: E=Easy, M=Moderate, S=Strenuous

Suitable for Children	Dogs Allowed	Fees	Swimming	Primitive Access Roads	Historical Interest
✔	✔	✔	✔		✔
✔					
✔	✔				
✔		✔		✔	
✔	✔	✔	✔	✔	
✔	✔	✔	✔	✔	
✔		✔	✔		✔
✔	✔				
✔	✔			✔	✔
✔	✔			✔	
✔		✔	✔	✔	
✔	✔		✔	✔	
✔	✔				
✔	✔				
✔	✔				
✔	✔		✔	✔	
✔			✔		
✔		✔	✔		✔

CHAPTER ONE

Vineyard Haven—Oak Bluffs— Edgartown Loop

Eye-popping panoramas just keep on coming—from Lagoon Pond in Vineyard Haven to the headwall overlooking Nantucket Sound at East Chop in Oak Bluffs, and along the barrier beach beside Sengekontacket Pond. Swimming is possible at any point on the 2-mile-long Sylvia State Beach. This loop also runs by four explorations described in other chapters and can be linked with the Chappaquiddick, State Forest, Vineyard Haven, and Katama rides.

Distance: 16.4 miles.

Difficulty: Easy. Bike paths run along 11.5 miles of the route. There is no path connecting Vineyard Haven and Oak Bluffs.

Stops along the way: Camp Meeting Grounds, Edgartown–Lighthouse Beach, Caroline Tuthill Wildlife Preserve, Felix Neck Wildlife Sanctuary, Manuel Correllus State Forest.

Food and drink: Vineyard Haven, near the Steamship Authority terminal: Black Dog Bakery, A & P supermarket, Mad Martha's; in the Tisbury Market

Place on Beach Road: SodaPops, Mystic Grill; in Oak Bluffs, on New York Avenue, east of the harbor: Mad Martha's.

Restrooms: Vineyard Haven: at the rear of the Steamship Authority terminal; Oak Bluffs: north of the Steamship Authority's dock on Beach Road.

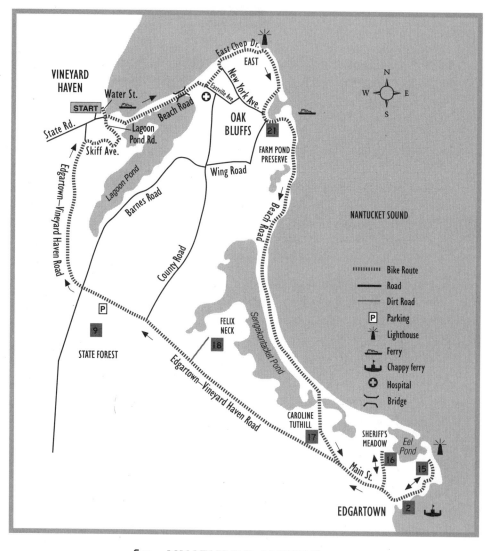

🚲 VINEYARD HAVEN–
OAK BLUFFS–EDGARTOWN LOOP

THE ROUTE

1. Begin at the Steamship Authority terminal at the end of Union Street in Vineyard Haven. Because of heavy traffic, I suggest walking your bike to Water Street and then turning left.

2. Continue walking your bike past the Black Dog Bakery on the left and the A & P across the street. Both stores can supply you with food and drink to take on your ride. At the busy Five Corners intersection, bear left onto Beach Road, heading toward Oak Bluffs.

    A narrow bike lane and a short bike path on this 1.5-mile stretch offer some protection from the traffic.

    On the right is the Tisbury Market Place. The Mystic Grill and SodaPops sell food and drink. Soon after, on the right lies Wind's Up, a water-sports store where you can learn how to kayak or wind-surf on Lagoon Pond.

    Beach Road becomes a causeway, crossing Vineyard Haven Harbor on the left and Lagoon Pond on the right. The Vietnam Veterans Memorial Bridge at the end of the causeway marks the boundary between the towns of Vineyard Haven and Oak Bluffs. If your timing is right, you won't have to wait for the drawbridge to open so that boats can travel between the pond and the harbor. When a hurricane or nor'easter is forecast, boats line up in the harbor to pass under the bridge to wait out the storm in Lagoon Pond.

    You can stop for your first swim just after the drawbridge, at **Eastville Point Beach**, the small sandy spit on your left that juts into Vineyard Haven Harbor.

3. After cycling by the hospital on the right, take your next left, following the sign to Oak Bluffs.

4. Take the first left (careful, a dangerous turn) onto East Chop Drive, following the sign to East Chop.

    On Martha's Vineyard, there are two "chops"—East and West. Here "chop" refers to an opening to a body of water. Both chops rise high above Vineyard Sound, protecting the entrances to Vineyard Haven and Oak Bluffs Harbors.

    As you bike along Highland Drive, look to your right at **Crystal Lake**, formerly known as Ice House Pond. Before the advent of refrigeration, residents used ice from this pond to keep their food from spoiling.

Proceed to the **East Chop Lighthouse**, perched high on Telegraph Hill, where you can dismount and enjoy the panorama. To the left lies West Chop, at the tip of Vineyard Haven. Falmouth, a town on the southern edge of Cape Cod, is the land mass far beyond.

Continue your loop around the bluff. For a panoramic view of Edgartown, Chappaquiddick, and then Cape Poge, stop just after you pass Atlantic Avenue on the right. The bluff provides an excellent vantage point for observing the activity below. Ferries from Hyannis, Falmouth, and Woods Hole continually shuttle passengers back and forth. Although small, the **Oak Bluffs Harbor** claims never to turn a boat away, so there is a constant stream of pleasure crafts motoring in and out.

As you proceed around the chop, just before the opening to the harbor, on the left, sits the East Chop Beach Club, a swimming, sailing, and tennis complex for families who summer on East Chop.

5. At the T intersection with Lake Avenue, turn left. Follow Lake past Oak Bluffs Harbor and Mad Martha's. If you wish to visit the **Camp Meeting Grounds** (chapter 21), proceed from this point.

6. Continue straight, heading toward the ocean and ferry terminal as Lake Avenue becomes one-way.

7. Turn right onto Seaview Avenue. The Steamship Authority terminal is on the left. The bike path begins in 0.6 mile, when the name of the road changes to Beach Road.

As you leave Oak Bluffs Center, you'll pass two parks: the first, **Ocean Park,** hosts summer band concerts and the annual fireworks display. After passing the second, **Waban Park,** you'll come to Farm Pond, home to two metal sea serpents perched in the middle of the pond. **Farm Pond Preserve,** a twenty-seven-acre property owned by the Martha's Vineyard Land Bank, occupies the land at the midpoint of the pond. A trail winds through marsh grass to the water.

Harthaven, a little community located south of the pond, is named after its settlers, the Harts. Look to your left for Harthaven's tiny harbor.

Since you travel straight on this road until you reach the center of Edgartown, you do not have to worry about missing a turn. However, be wary of other cyclists. Because this route is flat and skirts spectacular shoreline, it is the most popular path on the island. Not everyone knows the rules of the road, so stay right and remain alert.

A section of the **Farm Neck Golf Course** abuts the bike path. Because of the gorgeous views from many of its holes, Farm Neck is regarded as the most scenic course on the island.

Just ahead is the beginning of the **Joseph A. Sylvia State Beach**. Early morning swimmers frequent this beach for daily exercise. Windsurfers also favor this beach because of its calm seas and steady winds. In mid-afternoon, when the wind picks up, the more adventurous windsurfers jump on their boards.

Less adventurous windsurfers attempt the sport on the other side of the road in the less intimidating Sengekontacket Pond. If the tide is low, windsurfers may be joined by clammers, since the pond supports an abundance of shellfish. In autumn the pond is a popular scalloping spot.

If you decide to stop and swim, you can park your cycle in a bike rack in a small parking lot on the left side of the road, at the southeast end of the beach.

During late spring and early summer a common island shrub, **_Rosa rugosa_**, flaunts its delicate pink blossoms. This sun-loving plant thrives in sandy soil and is commonly found along roads and beaches. In the fall the blossoms become shiny, red, round hips, which are a great source of vitamin C.

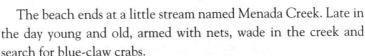

Rosa rugosa

The beach ends at a little stream named Menada Creek. Late in the day young and old, armed with nets, wade in the creek and search for blue-claw crabs.

8. After cycling 5 miles from the Steamship Authority terminal, you will reach the intersection of Beach Road and Edgartown–Vineyard Haven

Cannonball Park, the beginning of your trip through Edgartown and environs.

Road. The intersection forms a wedge called the Great Harbor Triangle, which hosts a variety of shops and a few restaurants.

To reach Cannonball Park, where the **Edgartown** (chapter 15) **Sheriff's Meadow Sanctuary** (chapter 16) walks and the Chappaquiddick bike ride (chapter 2) depart, continue straight onto what is now called Upper Main Street. **Cannonball Park** is wedged between the convergence of Upper Main Street, Cooke Street, and the Edgartown–West Tisbury Road.

9. To continue the loop and/or to visit the Caroline Tuthill Wildlife Preserve and Felix Neck Wildlife Sanctuary, turn right at the bicycle sign into the Great Harbor Triangle parking lot.

10. Cross the Edgartown–Vineyard Haven Road and turn right onto the bike path for 6.5 miles to Vineyard Haven.

The obscured entrance to the **Caroline Tuthill Wildlife Preserve** (chapter 17) is located on the right side of the Edgartown–Vineyard Haven Road, 0.5 mile from the Beach Road intersection just after Hamlen Way on the left and across from a stucco house at No. 346. Within the preserve, which sits on the shore of Sengekontacket Pond, is a trail that loops for 1.4 miles through 154 acres of woodland.

One and a half miles farther, on the right, lies the **Felix Neck Wildlife Sanctuary** (chapter 18), a 350-acre preserve maintained by the Massachusetts Audubon Society. More than a hundred species of birds have been observed in and around this sanctuary.

Less than a mile from the entrance to Felix Neck sits the entrance to a subdivision known as Dodger's Hole, named after the glacial kettle hole that can be seen through the clearing about 300 feet beyond Dodger's Hole Road. **Dodger's Hole** was formed about fifteen thousand years ago, after the glacier that covered Martha's Vineyard began to melt and recede. A large block of ice separated from the glacier and became buried in the earth, leaving a very large hole when it melted. Because this deep hole lay below the water table, it formed a pond. Dodger's Hole is rapidly drying up, however, and is now more bog than pond.

One mile from Dodger's Hole Road is Martha's Vineyard Regional High School. Sanderson Avenue, the access road to the **Manuel F. Correllus State Forest,** lies between the school building and the playing fields. The starting point for the State Forest East off-road bike ride (chapter 9) is 1 mile down the access road.

Just ahead, at the intersection with Barnes Road is the "blinker," the only traffic light on the island. Of course, there are other intersections that could use a traffic light, but Vineyarders balk at any mechanized reminder of the mainland.

Thimble Farm, on the left 0.4 mile from the blinker and 0.5 mile west on Stoney Hill Road, grows strawberries and raspberries which are available for picking from 10:00 A.M. to 5:00 P.M. throughout the summer. The owners also grow tomatoes hydroponically and have computerized the entire process. The temperature and amount of water, sunlight, and fertilizer are all computer controlled.

11. After the bike path ends, cross the Edgartown–Vineyard Haven Road and pedal toward Vineyard Haven. Continue 0.4 mile and take the third right onto Skiff Avenue. This maneuver not only escapes the traffic heading into Vineyard Haven Center but also has a great downhill run.

12. Turn left at the T intersection onto Lagoon Pond Road.

13. Carefully cross at Five Corners to Water Street. Head down Water to your starting point at the Steamship Authority terminal.

CHAPTER TWO

Chappaquiddick

Chappaquiddick is perfect for biking: flat terrain, little traffic, and no routing hassles. Since there is only one paved road, it's almost impossible to get lost. "Chappy" also offers mellow off-road cycling so you can alternate pavement with pine-needle-covered paths.

In order to get to Chappaquiddick, you must hop on the ferry that runs continually between Edgartown and Chappaquiddick, an Indian word meaning "separated island." Once you reach Chappy, you'll discover there is not much happening. Its residents enjoy the outdoor life and prefer the absence of commercial activity.

During your ride you can stop to swim at Chappy Point Beach, East Beach, and/or Wasque Reservation, as well as explore five conservation areas on bike or foot.

Distance: 12.8 miles round-trip from Cannonball Park.

Difficulty: Easy, flat terrain. The last mile is unpaved and sandy.

Stops along the way: Brine's Pond Preserve, Mytoi, East Beach, Chappy Five Corners Preserve, Poucha Pond Reservation, Wasque Reservation.

Fees: Wasque Reservation.

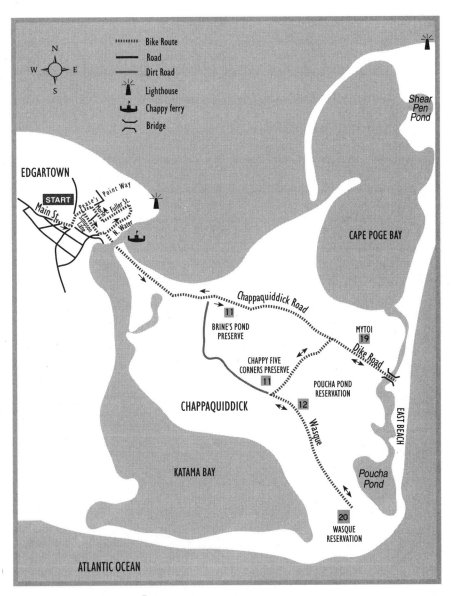

Map legend:
- .... Bike Route
- —— Road
- - - - Dirt Road
- Lighthouse
- Chappy ferry
- Bridge

N / W / E / S (compass)

EDGARTOWN
START
Main St.
Pease's Point Way
Morse
Fuller St.
Simpson Lne.
N. Water

Shear Pen Pond

CAPE POGE BAY

Chappaquiddick Road

11 BRINE'S POND PRESERVE

MYTOI 19
Dike Road

CHAPPY FIVE CORNERS PRESERVE 11

POUCHA POND RESERVATION

CHAPPAQUIDDICK

12 Wasque

EAST BEACH

KATAMA BAY

Poucha Pond

20 WASQUE RESERVATION

ATLANTIC OCEAN

🚲 CHAPPAQUIDDICK LOOP

Food and drink: Edgartown: Village Market and Rotisserie, 199 Main Street, next to the Mobil station and across from the western tip of Cannonball

Park; Soigné, gourmet takeout, 190 Main Street, at the junction of Cooke and Main. Chappaquiddick: Chappy General Store, located on the left side, 2.2 miles from the ferry landing. You can refill your water bottle at the hand pump at Wasque Reservation or at the water fountain in Mytoi.

Restrooms: Edgartown: on the left side of the Visitor Center on Church Street, located between Main Street and Pease's Point Way; Chappaquiddick: at Mytoi, East Beach, and Wasque Reservation.

Background: Chappaquiddick was inhabited by the Wampanoag Tribe long before European settlers arrived. These Native Americans used simple tools to work the land and subsisted on such foods as corn and shellfish. In cold weather they lived inland, moving near the ocean when the temperature rose.

The English arrived in 1642 and soon began to use the land on Chappaquiddick for grazing sheep and cattle. In October of each year, the farmers drove their livestock to an area close to Chappy Five Corners Preserve, where the animals would spend the winter. Come spring, the sheep were herded to a pond in Cape Poge Bay, where they were washed and shorn of their wool. This pond continues to bear the name Shear Pen Pond, reflecting how it was used three hundred years ago.

European settlers did not reside on Chappy until the middle of the eighteenth century, when Edgartown became a major whaling port. At that time, a lighthouse was erected on Cape Poge to guide ships into the busy Edgartown harbor, and ship captains began to move to Chappaquiddick. By 1878 there were forty-two settlers living on the island. However, it wasn't until the end of the nineteenth century that vacationers began to summer here.

Because of Chappy's limited access, most people were not aware of its physical attributes until 1969, when Senator Edward Kennedy's car drove off Dike Bridge. This highly publicized tragedy drew throngs of people searching for "The Bridge." Some of these visitors discovered that Dike Bridge leads to East Beach, a glorious 5-mile-long barrier beach. Chappaquiddick's new notoriety, combined with the 1970s building boom, created a demand for homes which produced the first surge of population growth in a hundred years. Even today, many people continue to associate this little island with the Kennedy tragedy rather than with its other considerable physical assets.

THE ROUTE

1. From Cannonball Park (also known as Memorial Park), the wedge of land formed by the junction of Upper Main Street, Cooke Street, and the Edgartown–West Tisbury Road, proceed east on Main Street toward Edgartown Center.

2. Pedal two blocks and turn left onto Pease's Point Way, following the Bike Route signs.

3. Turn right, remaining on Pease's Point Way, following the signs to the Chappy ferry.

4. Proceed two blocks past the bicycle parking area on Pease's Point Way until you reach Simpson Lane (the road on the left side is named Pierce Lane). Turn right, following the Bike Route and Chappy Ferry signs.

5. Proceed two blocks to North Water Street and turn left.

6. Immediately turn right onto Daggett Street. The Chappy Ferry signs are clearly posted at this turn.

7. Ride down the short stretch to the ferry landing. The cars parked to your right are in line for the ferry; however, bikers do not have to wait. Park your bike to the right of the loading platform, where there may be an attendant to collect fees ($3 round-trip for cyclists; no money is collected on the return trip). Wait until cars, bikers, and pedestrians disembark. After the two-minute ferry ride, the attendant will indicate when to get off.

    Chappy Point Beach, to the left of the ferry slip, offers a great view of Edgartown Harbor. Here you can look at the parade of boats motoring in and out of Katama Bay, with stately Edgartown residences in the background.

8. Proceed 1.5 miles from the ferry to **Brine's Pond Preserve,** identified by a tree-covered island sitting in a small pond on the right side of the road (an off-road biking route, described in chapter 11).

    The Chappy General Store, which carries a little of everything, is located on the left side 0.5 mile from Brine's Pond.

9. At 0.5 mile past the Chappy General Store, the paved road swings sharply right. To reach **Mytoi** and **East Beach** (chapter 19), continue straight onto the dirt road. Mytoi lies 0.5 mile down the road. East Beach is 0.2 mile farther.

To continue the ride, remain on the paved road for 0.8 mile until you reach the junction with Wasque Road.

Chappy Five Corners Preserve (chapter 11) is nestled in the right corner. Across the road from the preserve lies a large boulder etched with the words Blow Your Bugle. Island lore attributes the directive to the previous owner of the land, whose children had the stone carved in his memory.

10. Turn left onto Wasque Road. Continue 0.5 mile to **Poucha Pond Reservation** (chapter 12), on the left immediately after the second 25 MPH speed-limit sign. You can explore the reservation on bike or foot.

    Soon after Poucha Pond Reservation, a mile-long stretch of stony, rutted, sandy road begins. To best navigate this road, shift into a low gear so that your bike wheels will spin and give better traction. Keep your wheels straight to keep your bike from skidding on the sand. When you encounter soft, sandy sections, you may have to dismount and walk your bike until the surface becomes firmer.

    If you decide to explore **Wasque Reservation** (chapter 20), you will receive a monetary award for negotiating this challenging road on bike—you won't have to pay the $3 automobile entrance fee, but during the summer season you will have to pay $3 per person to swim, hike, or bike.

11. To return, proceed down Wasque Road. Turn right onto School Road.

12. At the junction with Chappaquiddick Road, bear left for the 2.5-mile ride back to the On Time ferry, so-named because two ferries cross the short distance between Chappaquiddick and Edgartown in minutes, ensuring that one of the ferries is always at each shore.

13. After disembarking from the ferry, you must walk your bike up Daggett Street (one way) to North Water Street. Turn right.

    The houses on the left side of North Water Street were built at an angle so that their occupants—families of captains of whaling ships—would have a better view of the boats sailing into the harbor. After you pass Morse Street, look up onto the roof of the second house on the left. The balustrade on the top, called a "widow's walk," enabled a captain's wife to look far out onto the ocean as she anxiously awaited her husband's return.

Just before the road bends, look to your right at the **Edgartown Lighthouse**. The original lighthouse was built in 1828 on a small man-made island 0.25 mile out into the harbor. One could only gain access to it by boat. However, the next year a footbridge was built. In 1938 the structure was replaced, but by then it no longer sat on an island, since ocean currents had created a sandbar between the lighthouse and the mainland. A mile-long public beach extends from the lighthouse to Eel Pond.

14. Continue around the bend and turn left on Fuller Street. Colorful gardens decorate the side yards of these attractive old homes.

15. Fuller ends at Morse Street. Turn right.

16. Take your second left onto Pease's Point Way.

17. Follow Pease's Point Way as it bends around and intersects Main Street. Turn right.

18. Remain on Main Street to return to Cannonball Park.

CHAPTER THREE

Katama Point—South Beach

Whataday! Sunny, balmy—perfect beach weather—an excellent opportunity for a ride to a 3-mile stretch of sandy beach pounded by crashing waves. A trip to Katama Point and South Beach, located at the southeastern tip of Martha's Vineyard, offers a great ride, much of it on bike paths, as well as a cool, scenic destination. A big advantage to biking is that you won't have to search for a place to park at one of the most popular beaches on Martha's Vineyard. Forget about cycling in your bathing suit; South Beach has a bathhouse.

Distance: 23.3 miles round-trip from the ferry terminal in Vineyard Haven.

Difficulty: Easy.

Stops along the way: Felix Neck Wildlife Sanctuary, Caroline Tuthill Wildlife Preserve, State Forest East, Katama Point Preserve.

Food and drink: Vineyard Haven: Union Street, Black Dog Bakery, A & P; on the Edgartown–Vineyard Haven Road: Norton Farm; Edgartown: Upper Main Street, A & P, Dairy Queen, and The Fresh Pasta Shoppe; on corner of Edgartown–West Tisbury and Meshacket Roads, Morning Glory Farm.

Restrooms: Vineyard Haven: in the ferry terminal building; Edgartown: next to the bathhouse at the entrance to South Beach.

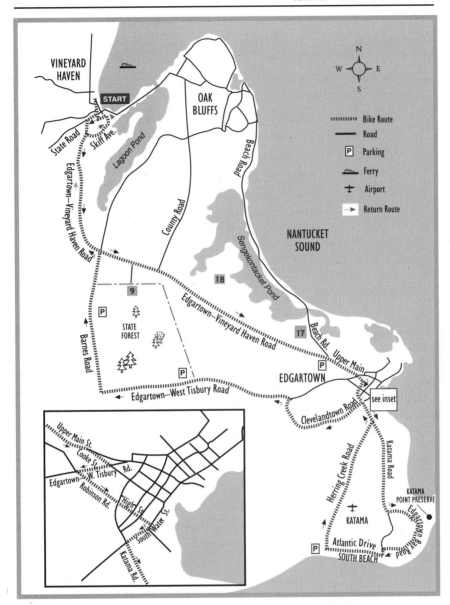

🚲FROM VINEYARD HAVEN TO KATAMA POINT

THE ROUTE

Oak Bluffs bikers: Follow the directions in the West Tisbury South Loop chapter to the intersection of County Road and the Edgartown–Vineyard Haven Road. Turn left toward Edgartown and pick up the directions at No. 6.

Edgartown bikers: Begin the following directions at No. 8.

1. From the Steamship Authority dock on Union Street, take the first left onto Water Street.

    The A & P supermarket and the Black Dog Bakery are coveniently located for stocking up for the trip. You also will pass many other restaurants and stores on the Edgartown–Vineyard Haven Road in Edgartown.

2. Hook a right through the A & P parking lot, which leads to Main Street. (This maneuver is called "cutting off crowded corners").

3. Turn left onto Main. You will have to walk your bike, since Main is a one-way street.

4. Main ends at State Road. Turn right and continue walking your bike up this short, steep, congested stretch.

5. Turn left onto the Edgartown–Vineyard Haven Road toward Edgartown. The bike path begins in 0.6 mile and continues for 6.6 miles.

    If you want to purchase fresh produce, Norton Farm is 1.4 miles up the road. The **Martha's Vineyard Community Services** complex is located 1.2 miles east of Norton Farm. The buildings house such services as early-childhood programs, a counseling center, and substance abuse and emergency psychiatric services.

    The wooded area across from Community Services and behind the Martha's Vineyard Regional High School is the 4,343-acre **Manuel F. Correllus State Forest**, half of which lies in Edgartown, the other half in West Tisbury. Sanderson Avenue, the entrance road to the forest and the starting point for the State Forest East off-road bike ride (chapter 9), runs next to the high school.

    Two miles from the high school on the left side is **Felix Neck Wildlife Sanctuary** (chapter 18), a great place for youngsters to walk trails as well as to view exhibits and wildlife.

    Another area with easy walking trails is the **Caroline Tuthill Wildlife Preserve** (chapter 17) located on the left 1.5 miles past Felix Neck.

6. The Edgartown–Vineyard Haven Road intersects with Beach Road, forming a wedge of land called the Great Harbor Triangle, filled with

shops and restaurants. At the intersection of the two roads, the street name changes to Upper Main Street. Continue on Upper Main past the commercial establishments.

7. At the fork bear right onto the bike path on Cooke Street, following the signs to Katama and South Beach. On the left side of Cooke Street sits Cannonball Park, the departure point for explorations that begin in Edgartown.

8. Take the first right onto the Edgartown–West Tisbury Road.

9. Turn left onto Robinson Road, following the sign to Katama. Bike past the elementary school on the left, and the parking lot and bus stop on the right.

> In order to reduce automobile traffic, Edgartown runs a free shuttle bus to the business district. The town also operates a trolley to South Beach. Behind the parking lot lies the Edgartown recreation area, with playing fields and tennis courts.

10. Continue through the next intersection onto High Street, following the South Beach Bike Route signs.

11. Follow High Street for three blocks to the T intersection with South Water Street. Turn right.

12. Remain on South Water to the first intersection, Katama Road. Turn left.

13. Proceed on the bike path on Katama Road for 2 miles to Edgartown Bay Road. Turn left.

14. This road loops, paralleling Katama Bay. Proceed on this road for 0.7 mile. Look on your left for the partially hidden Land Bank logo sign and Katama Point Preserve. If you reach the town-landing parking lot, you have gone too far and should go back 750 feet.

> **Katama Point Preserve**, a two-acre parcel of land owned by the Land Bank Commission, sits on Katama Bay. The point juts out into the water, offering an extended view of Edgartown and its harbor as well as the southern end of Chappaquiddick. Here birdwatchers spot shorebirds such as cormorants, least terns, and the osprey family nesting on a pole in the center of the property.

If you wish to visit the preserve, park your bike in the bike rack and head down the trail toward the water. You'll spot the osprey pole on the left. Since the installation of these poles, there has been a recent insurgence in ospreys , which are fish-catching hawks. The island osprey population had diminished due to a lack of dead trees, which are the natural nesting sites of ospreys. Volunteers working in conjunction with the telephone company installed telephone poles all over the island to provide safe nesting sites. As you explore the island, you'll notice other nesting poles.

Continue on to the beach. Because Katama Point protrudes into Katama Bay, you are able to see miles of Edgartown coastline, including its harbor (Katama Bay is explored by kayak in chapter 33). Directly ahead lies Chappaquiddick, commonly referred to as an island. However, if you look to your right, you will see that Chappaquiddick is actually connected to the Vineyard by a 2-mile-long stretch of barrier beach. Chappaquiddick has been an island only ten times in the last 200 years, when violent storms created an opening in the barrier beach, allowing the ocean to flow into Katama Bay.

Picnicking, fishing, and swimming are permitted here, but if you prefer a larger sandy beach and surf, return on the same trail to pick up your bike and continue on to South Beach.

15.   At Edgartown Bay Road, turn left toward the entrance to South Beach.

Bike racks line the road near its intersection with Atlantic Drive. North of the road lies Mattakeesett Herring Creek, a man-made ditch that connects Katama Bay to Edgartown Great Pond. The original Herring Creek was created in 1728 and drew 700,000 herring which swam here annually to spawn. This second Herring Creek was excavated at the end of the nineteenth century to replace the first one, which because of erosion now lies about a mile out in the ocean. Early Vineyard maps show a series of freshwater ponds that also have been swallowed up by the sea. Rumor has it that Vineyarders used to ice-skate from Katama Bay to Edgartown Great Pond on these interconnected ponds.

If you wish to visit South Beach, park your bike and walk onto the beach. Over the last eighteen years, I have noticed a marked diminution in the width of the beach. The reason: the ocean is encroaching on the south coast at an annual rate of 8 feet a year. As you walk, you'll notice some sections of beach have been totally swept away, leaving only sand dunes.

If you are seeking solitude, head east toward Chappaquiddick. The farther you walk, the fewer people you'll see. Four-wheel-drive vehicles can reach these remote sections by driving in through the motorists' entrance, located to the left of the main entrance. Drivers must buy a permit and be able to navigate a narrow sandy strip that extends 3 miles to Wasque Point. Vehicles are not allowed on the beach when baby piping plovers and least terns are in residence.

This eastern section of beach parallels Katama Bay; you can either walk by the surf or along the edge of the bay. Be careful when you cross from the ocean side to the bay to avoid walking on the fragile sand dunes. Dunes help to slow beach erosion; the higher they are, the less the ocean can encroach on the land.

Sandpiper

Least terns, which look like skinny sea gulls, often nest in this section. In order to protect the diminishing tern population, conservationists have roped off their nesting areas.

In this remote section you'll be more likely to spot **sandpipers**, tiny birds with long bills, who appear to be racing back and forth on the sand chasing each receding wave. What they are really doing is searching for sand fleas that emerge from little openings in the wet sand to feed on plankton carried in by the surf.

If you want to swim, head back to the mile-long, lifeguard-supervised section of the beach. If the waves are high, there often will be a strong undertow. Rip tides, strong currents that flow rapidly away from shore, occasionally have trapped unsuspecting swimmers.

Lifeguards advise swimmers caught in the rip to swim at a right angle to the flow, parallel to the shore, until out of the current.

16. When you are ready to leave the beach, retrieve your bike and turn left onto Atlantic Drive.

17. Atlantic Drive runs for 1 mile to Herring Creek Road, the second entrance road to South Beach. Turn right. There is no bike path on this 2-mile stretch, but the road is straight and is not as busy as Katama Road.

    On the right you will pass Katama Air Park, a grassy landing field for small private planes and gliders.

    Ahead on the right is the twenty-eight-acre Waller Farm, purchased jointly by the town of Edgartown and the Land Bank Commission in order to preserve island farmland.

18. At the intersection with Katama Road turn left.

19. Take your first major left onto Clevelandtown Road. This road curves around for 1.8 miles and changes its name in the middle to Meshacket Road. It passes the town dump and then Morning Glory Farm, which has a farmstand located on the corner of the Edgartown–West Tisbury Road where you can buy fresh produce and baked goods.

20. Turn left onto the bike path on the Edgartown–West Tisbury Road.

21. Continue on the path for 1.4 miles until the path crosses from the south to the north side of the road. The path continues for another 1.7 miles to Barnes Road.

22. Turn right onto Barnes Road. The bike path is on the left side of this road and is hidden from view.

23. Pedal for 2.4 miles to the "blinker," the only traffic light on Martha's Vineyard. Turn left on the Edgartown–Vineyard Haven Road toward Vineyard Haven.

24. After the bike path ends, cross to the right side of the road, proceed 0.4 mile, and take your third right onto Skiff Avenue.

25. Enjoy the downhill, enhanced by a view of Lagoon Pond. Turn left at the end of the descent onto Lagoon Pond Road.

26. Lagoon Pond Road joins four other roads at the hazardous Five Corners intersection. Walk your bike across the road, then continue on Water Street.

27. At Union Street you can either turn right toward the ferry dock or turn left toward Mad Martha's for an ice cream.

CHAPTER FOUR

Vineyard Haven—West Chop— Herring Creek Beach

This trip explores Vineyard Haven, the busiest port on Martha's Vineyard, and then follows the coastline north to West Chop for sweeping views of Vineyard Sound, Cape Cod, and the Elizabeth Islands. The grand finale is a visit to Herring Creek Beach, a picturesque peninsula where you can wade in the calm waters of Lake Tashmoo or swim in Vineyard Sound. Since automobile parking is limited, Herring Creek Beach is perfect for cyclists who don't mind pedaling over a mile-long unpaved, and often sandy, road.

Distance: 16.6 miles round-trip (20 miles with the side trip to Herring Creek Beach) from the ferry terminal in Oak Bluffs.

Difficulty: Easy, flat terrain with little traffic; 6.7 miles of bike paths; unpaved road to Herring Creek Beach.

Stops along the way: Eastville Point Beach, Jirah Luce House, Captain Richard C. Luce House, Association Hall, Old Schoolhouse, Owen Park, Association Hall Cemetery.

Food and drink: Across from the Steamship Authority on Seaview Avenue in Oak Bluffs: Oak Bluffs General Store, Lookout Tavern; Tisbury Market Place on Beach Road: Soda Pops, Mystic Grill.

Restrooms: Oak Bluffs: next to the Steamship Authority terminal on Seaview Avenue;
Vineyard Haven: in the Steamship Authority terminal on Union Street.

Background: Because of the variation in posted signs, visitors can be confused by the two names for this town. Is it Vineyard Haven or Tisbury? Vineyard Haven is actually incorporated into the town of Tisbury, but residents differentiate between the two names by referring to the business district and harbor as Vineyard Haven and the surrounding area as Tisbury.

Vineyard Haven was settled in 1674, and its original name was Holmes Hole. "Hole" referred to the location of its harbor, protected by the two headlands of East Chop and West Chop. Holmes may have been the name of the owner of the adjoining land.

Although Holmes Hole began as a farming community, its protected location on Vineyard Sound destined it to become a popular seaport. By the middle of the nineteenth century, the harbor was second only to the English Channel in the number of ships that stopped on their way to and from Europe, Africa, and the West Indies.

Vineyard Haven thrived, catering to thousands of vessels that harbored in its port. Many residents became pilots and accompanied these ships on their journeys. Others provided sails, navigation equipment, food, and clothing. However, the opening of the Cape Cod Canal in 1914, combined with the increased use of trains, trucks, and steamships to move cargo, reduced the number of vessels passing through Vineyard Sound. Vineyard Haven continues to be the island center for commercial sea traffic, but now its ferries carry the cargo that drives the island's main industry—tourism.

THE ROUTE

Edgartown bikers: Follow the Edgartown–Vineyard Haven Road to its intersection with State Road in Vineyard Haven. Turn left and pick up the directions at No. 9.

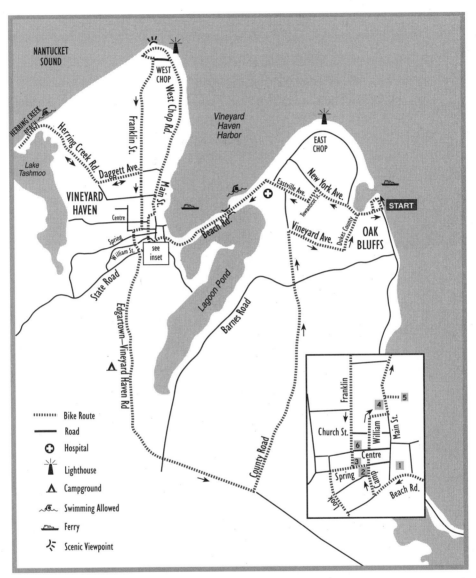

NANTUCKET
SOUND

WEST
CHOP

West Chop Rd.

Franklin St.

HERRING CREEK BEACH

Herring Creek Rd.

Lake
Tashmoo

Daggett Ave.

VINEYARD
HAVEN

Centre

Spring

William St.

State Road

Main St.

see
inset

Vineyard
Haven
Harbor

EAST
CHOP

New York Ave.

Eastville Ave.

Tuwanticut St.

Beach Rd.

Vineyard Ave.

Dukes County

OAK
BLUFFS

START

Edgartown—Vineyard Haven Rd

Lagoon Pond

Barnes Road

County Road

- - - - - - - Bike Route
——— Road
✚ Hospital
☀ Lighthouse
⛺ Campground
⛵ Swimming Allowed
⛴ Ferry
🏃 Scenic Viewpoint

Franklin

Church St.

William

Main St.

6

4

5

Centre

3

2

Spring

Camp

Look

1

Beach Rd.

🚲VINEYARD HAVEN—WEST CHOP—HERRING CREEK BEACH

Vineyard Haven bikers: From the Steamship Authority terminal, take the first left on Water Street. At the Five Corners intersection turn right, and pick up the directions at No. 7.

1. Begin at the Steamship Authority terminal on Seaview Avenue in Oak Bluffs.

2. Turn right on Seaview Avenue and head toward the parking area for cabs, buses, and cars waiting for the Island Queen and Hy-Line ferries.

3. At the parking lot, turn left and pedal to the main road, New York Avenue.

4. Turn right onto New York Avenue, pedal past Oak Bluffs Harbor, and proceed for 0.8 mile (1 mile total) to Towanticut Street. Turn left toward Vineyard Haven.

5. Take your first right on Eastville Avenue, following the signs toward the Martha's Vineyard Hospital and Vineyard Haven.

6. Continue straight on Eastville as it passes Martha's Vineyard Hospital and then hooks a sharp left and becomes Beach Road.

    Having pedaled a grand total of 2 miles, you may wish to stop for a swim at Eastville Point Beach on the right side, just before the drawbridge.

    Remain on Beach Road for 1 mile, pedaling over the drawbridge that spans Lagoon Pond on the left and Vineyard Haven Harbor on the right. Just past the bridge, on the left, lies a boat-launching area. Just beyond, a bike path runs for 0.3 mile to the Tisbury Market Place, where you can stop for food and drink.

7. Soon after passing the Tisbury Market Place, you will enter the Five Corners intersection. Turn left and walk your bike up Beach Road.

    The **Jirah Luce House** (1) sits on the right side of Beach Road. The building, built in 1804, was one of the few that survived the fire of 1883, which destroyed most of the buildings in the center.

8. Continue walking up Beach Road. Pass Main and take the first right onto narrow Camp Street.

9. Camp is one way, so continue walking your bike up the short hill to the intersection with William Street.

    The handsome **Captain Richard C. Luce House** (2) at 40 William Street sits directly across from Camp Street. It was built in 1833 for Luce, one of the Vineyard's most successful whaling captains. This Greek Revival–style home was the first of its size to be built in Vineyard Haven. Soon other whaling captains followed Luce's lead and built homes on William Street.

10. Turn right on William Street.

11. Take the first left on Spring Street. Walk your bike (another one-way) to the third building on the right.

> **Association Hall** (3) was built in 1844 and served as a meeting-house and church for Baptists and Congregationalists. Now it functions as both the town hall and the Katherine Cornell Memorial Theatre. To commemorate Vineyard Haven's 300th anniversary, the actress Katherine Cornell donated funds to restore Association Hall and remodel its theater.

12. Return to William Street and turn left. Pedal past other Greek Revival–style captains' homes. This street, an officially designated historic district, was spared in 1883 because the fire moved downhill rather than up.

13. After pedaling four blocks (0.2 mile), turn right on tiny Colonial Lane (there may not be a street sign). Travel down Colonial Lane to Main.

> The **Old Schoolhouse** (4) is situated on the right corner. Its bell tower is the only remaining section of the original schoolhouse, which was built in 1829. The pole in front of the schoolhouse commemorates three colonial girls who defied British troops during a daring raid.

14. Turn left on Main Street.

15. Take your next right onto Owen Park Road.

> **Owen Park** (5) contains benches, swings, and a bandstand used during Sunday evening concerts. Continue down the road to the public beach if you wish to swim or rest while watching ferries shuttle in and out of the harbor.

16. Return to Main Street and turn right for the 2-mile ride to West Chop. The road loops around, following the coastline.

> **West Chop**, the Vineyard's northernmost headland, refers both to a geographical location on Martha's Vineyard and a self-contained community with its own beaches, tennis courts, and post office.
>
> West Chop's progression from a sheep pasture to resort community began in 1872. Two sea captains purchased a large tract of land for $400, and then managed to sell the same parcel a few weeks later for $10,000. Fifteen years later, the West Chop Land and Wharf Company turned the area into an exclusive summer resort, trans-

porting its residents from the mainland to the company's new wharf via steamboat. As you bike along the bluff, you'll see grand old gray-shingled cottages, many of which were built during this era.

Just before you reach the tip of the headland, you'll spot the **West Chop Lighthouse**, guardian of busy Vineyard Haven Harbor. The lighthouse was built and moved several times in its history. It began its career in 1817 as a wooden structure, which was rebuilt in brick in 1838. Erosion of the 60-foot bluff required the lighthouse be moved in 1848 and again in 1891.

Proceed until you are at the tip of West Chop (6 miles total). Look on the right for a clearing that contains a bench for cyclists to relax and enjoy the splendid panorama. The view from this northern point includes the Elizabeth Islands to the left. Woods

The historic lighthouse in West Chop.

Hole and Falmouth lie straight ahead. Because the distance between Woods Hole and the Elizabeth Islands is quite small, it often appears as if they are one big land mass. Along with pleasure crafts cruising on this busy waterway, you may spot one of the many ferry boats traveling between the island and the mainland.

17. Bend left around the point, passing the West Chop Tennis Club. At the fork bear right onto Franklin Street (there may not be a street sign at this point).

18. Remain on Franklin for 1.3 miles—passing the western edge of West Chop Woods and the entrance to Mink Meadows Golf Course on the right—to Daggett Street. It's easy to miss this turn because the street sign is on the left side of the road. Turn right on Daggett to proceed to Herring Creek Beach.

19. Follow Daggett for 0.5 mile to the Dead End sign. Turn right onto Herring Creek Road, a divided road for the first 0.5 mile. You do *not* want to continue straight into the Stonegate Lane subdivision.

Remain on Herring Creek Road for a 1.2 miles. Some sections are easier to navigate than others. Once you reach the peninsula, the dirt turns to sand. If shifting into a low gear to spin your wheels doesn't give you enough traction, you may have to walk your bike.

At **Herring Creek Beach** you can choose where to sun and swim. If you turn left, you'll head toward the shore of Lake Tashmoo. Be careful not to disturb the **least terns,** which may be nesting in the sand. Do not attempt to swim in the channel, where the water is deep and the current very strong. Do look across the channel to see if the eaglelike **osprey** is perched on a pole scanning the sea for a tasty tidbit. If it finds one, the osprey will land in the water feet first to gobble up its prey.

If you turn right, you'll soon be on the lifeguard-supervised stretch of sand adjacent to Vineyard Sound. From this beach you'll have the same spectacular panorama as at West Chop, including two of the Elizabeth Islands—the largest, Naushon, and tiny Nonamesset. You may also spot Woods Hole and Falmouth on Cape Cod.

20. After leaving Herring Creek Beach, retrace your ride on the dirt road.

21. Turn left on Daggett Street.

22. Ride down Daggett to Franklin and turn right.

Osprey

23. Remain on Franklin for eight blocks until you reach Center Street.

   The **Association Hill Cemetery** (6), at the corner of Franklin and Center Streets, displays stones that mark the graves of the Vineyard's English settlers. The oldest stone is dated 1770, but most represent the years from 1805 to 1817. To return to Oak Bluffs, continue on Franklin for another block.

24. Turn right onto Spring Street. (Since Spring is one-way, you must walk your bike one block—a worthwhile effort to avoid the congestion on State Road.)

25. Take the first left onto Look Street.

26. Remain on Look for two blocks until it ends at State Road. Cross State Road and head up the Edgartown–Vineyard Haven Road toward Edgartown.

27. Proceed on the Edgartown–Vineyard Haven Road for 3.3 miles, passing the "blinker" intersection. Turn left on County Road.

28. Continue on the bike path on County Road for 2.7 miles. At the four-way intersection with Barnes Road, the bike path crosses to the east side of the road. Turn right onto Vineyard Avenue.

30. Follow Vineyard Avenue until it ends at Dukes County Avenue. Turn left.

31. Remain on Dukes County Avenue until it ends at New York Avenue. Turn right.

32. Proceed straight to the ferry terminal.

CHAPTER FIVE

West Tisbury South Loop

Take a trip back in time, to when the Vineyard relied more on farming than tourism, by cycling through the agrarian center of the island, West Tisbury. This ride also offers opportunities for off-road biking, hiking, and swimming. Because the loop circumnavigates the forest, much of the pedaling is on bike paths.

Distance: Round-trip from the ferry terminal in Oak Bluffs, 25 miles.

Difficulty: Easy, mostly flat with a few short hills.

Stops along the way: Camp Meeting Grounds, Trade Wind Fields Preserve, State Forest East, State Forest West, Long Point Wildlife Refuge, Sepiessa Point Reservation, Agricultural Halls.

Food and drink: Oak Bluffs, across from the Steamship Authority Terminal on Seaview Avenue: Oak Bluffs General Store, Lookout Tavern; on Lake Avenue: Mad Martha's Ice Cream/Giant Grinders; West Tisbury on State Road: Alley's General Store, Back Alley's Café.

Restrooms: Oak Bluffs, next to the Steamship Authority terminal on Seaview Avenue.

Fees: Long Point Wildlife Refuge.

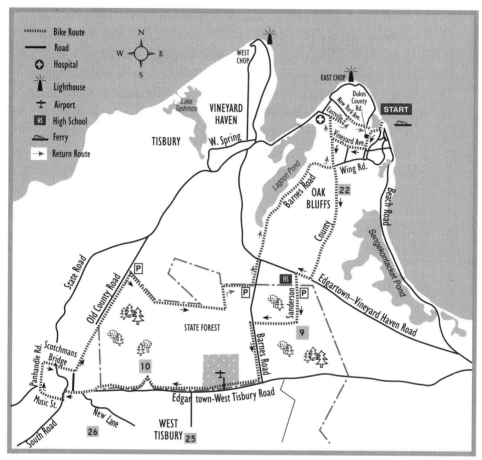

🚲 WEST TISBURY SOUTH LOOP

THE ROUTE

Edgartown bikers: Proceed west 4 miles on the Edgartown–Vineyard Haven Road to the Martha's Vineyard Regional High School. Turn left onto Sanderson Avenue, the road next to the school, and pick up the directions at No 7.

Vineyard Haven bikers: Follow the Edgartown–Vineyard Haven Road east for 2.7 miles to the Martha's Vineyard Regional High School. Turn right onto Sanderson Avenue and pick up the directions at No. 7.

1. Begin at the Oak Bluffs Steamship Authority terminal on Beach Road. Head down Oak Bluffs Avenue, the road in front of the terminal, to Lake Avenue.

2. Bear right on Lake Avenue.

3. Turn left onto Dukes County Avenue, across from Oak Bluffs Harbor.

    A small pond, Sunset Lake, is on your right. On your left lies the **Camp Meeting Grounds**, an enclave of historic Victorian-style homes circling the Tabernacle, described in chapter 21.

4. Take your fourth right onto Vineyard Avenue.

5. Follow Vineyard Avenue to the intersection with County Road. Turn left and join the bike path. Continue south through the stop-sign intersection with Barnes and Wing Roads, as the bike path changes to the right side of the road.

    A quarter-mile from the intersection, on the left, lies a large, grass airfield, a portion of the 71-acre **Trade Wind Fields Preserve** described in chapter 22. You can detour and take an easy 1.3-mile off-road bike ride.

6. Continue on County Road for 2 miles until it ends at the Edgartown–Vineyard Haven Road. Pedal onto the bike path and turn right (west).

7. The Martha's Vineyard Regional High School is 0.6 mile ahead on the left. Turn left onto Sanderson Avenue, the road that separates the playing field from the school. This road leads to the office of the superintendent of the 4,343-acre Manuel F. Corellus State Forest and the starting point for the **State Forest East** ride (chapter 9).

8. At the fork, bear right. Do not continue straight toward the state forest headquarters.

9. The road ends at Airport/Barnes Road. Cross the road to get on the dirt trail to the bike path (hidden from view) and turn left.

10. Continue on the bike path for 1.5 miles until you reach the junction with the Edgartown–West Tisbury Road. Remain on the bike path and turn right.

    The bike path continues for 3.6 miles, passing the entrance to the airport. An opening on the bike path to the Edgartown–West Tisbury Road (0.3 mile from the entrance to the airport) leads to the access road to **Long Point Wildlife Refuge** (chapter 25). The good news: Long

Point boasts a world-class beach. The bad news: you must ride 3 miles down a sandy road to reach it.

The bike path follows, with abrupt ascents and descents, the contour of the glacier-carved land. The **State Forest West** ride (chapter 10) begins just as the path heads into the forest and forms a V to avoid a wedge of privately owned land.

11.   Remain on the path as it passes the back entrance to Hostelling International. Just before the path makes a sharp right turn, a West Tisbury sign marks your left turn toward the Edgartown–West Tisbury Road.

12.   Turn right on the road toward West Tisbury Center, pedaling past the tiny fire station. To explore **Sepiessa Point Reservation** (chapter 26), turn left on New Lane, the first paved road after the fire station.

Grab a quick refreshment in Alley's General Store, established in 1858.

13. Just after Old Mill Pond, on the right, is the junction with South Road. Bear left toward West Tisbury Center.

   The inviting front porch of Alley's General Store appears on the right. Across the road is the Field Gallery, where sculptor Tom Maley's engaging figures frolic on the lawn.

   The **Old Agricultural Hall** sits on the corner of Music Street. On Saturday mornings and Wednesday afternoons, it hosts farmers and crafts people who sell their wares.

14. Take the next right onto Music Street. Remain on Music Street for 1.3 miles as the street forms a U.

   The farmland on this quiet country road is reminiscent of the island's agrarian past. The new **Agricultural Hall** sitting on the Martha's Vineyard Agricultural Society Grounds, 1 mile from the old hall, is the centerpiece of this agrarian tradition. The new hall and surrounding acreage contain the County Fair, one of the Vineyard's most popular events, which takes place the third week in August. Here log-rolling and oyster-shucking contests compete with dog shows, amusement park rides, food stands, booths, and displays including mammoth zucchinis and outstanding flower arrangements.

15. Remain on what is now called Panhandle Road as it crosses South Road. At the next intersection, Old County Road, turn left. Across the road sits one of the largest and most popular art houses, the Granary Gallery.

16. Proceed 1 mile on Old County Road. Turn right, passing by a brown barricade, into the forest to get on the bike path.

17. Turn left onto the bike path.

18. Continue on the path for 1 mile. After reaching the parking area, turn right onto the 2-mile path that travels east through the forest.

19. At the T intersection, turn left. The path runs north for a 0.5 mile and then turns east for another 0.5 mile.

20. Upon reaching another parking area, turn left onto the path that borders Barnes Road.

21. Remain on Barnes Road through its intersection with the Edgartown–Vineyard Haven Road. Barnes Road ascends and descends for 2.5 miles, occasionally offering views of Lagoon Pond on the left.

22. Turn left at the intersection with County Road and head onto the bike path on the right side of the road.

23. Remain on County Road to the T intersection with Eastville Avenue. Turn right toward Oak Bluffs.

24. Take your next left onto Towanticut Street.

25. Towanticut ends at New York Avenue. Turn right, and remain on New York Avenue for 1 mile.

26. To escape the traffic on your return to the Steamship Authority terminal, turn left just past the harbor onto the first side street.

27. Continue straight until the road/parking lot ends, then turn right onto Seaview Avenue. The terminal is ahead on the left.

CHAPTER SIX

West Tisbury North Loop

If you want a rural experience but don't have time for an up-island ride, try this short loop. Curving country roads, picturesque ponds for cooling off, and several hiking options contribute to this enjoyable exploration. Stops along the way include wine tours and tastings, berry picking, and, in the off-season, one of the most beautiful beaches on Martha's Vineyard.

Distance: From Vineyard Haven: 13.4 miles; for visits to Christiantown and Cedar Tree Neck add an additional 6 miles (2 miles are upaved).

Difficulty: Easy to moderate with a few hills, 1.4 miles of unpaved road; and only 2 miles of bike paths. Wear brightly colored clothing in order to be easily seen on shaded, narrow, curved roads.

Stops along the way: Ripley's Field Preserve, Duarte's Pond, Christiantown, Cedar Tree Neck Wildlife Sanctuary, Chicama Vineyard, Thimble Farm.

Food and drink: Vineyard Haven, near the ferry terminal: Mad Martha's Giant Grinders, Black Dog Bakery; on State Road: Black Dog Cafe; West Tisbury: Up-Island Cronig's, Biga Bakery.

Restrooms: In the Steamship Authority terminal in Vineyard Haven.

THE ROUTE

Edgartown bikers: Take the Edgartown–Vineyard Haven Road to the Steamship Authority Wharf in Vineyard Haven (Nos. 6, 7, and 8 in chapter 1).

Oak Bluffs bikers: Follow the directions in chapter 4 to Vineyard Haven.

1. Begin at the Martha's Vineyard Steamship Authority Wharf in Vineyard Haven, the main port of entry to the island. Crowds and cars disembarking from the ferry make it necessary to *walk* your bike straight up Union Street until you reach the intersection with Main Street.

2. Turn right onto Main Street.

3. Take a quick left on Church.

4. Now mount your bike and remain on Church for two blocks.

5. Turn left at Franklin for one block.

6. Turn right at Center Street.

7. At the T intersection, turn left at Pine Street.

8. Turn right on Spring Street and pass the Tisbury School.

9. At the fork bear right, and remain on West Spring Street for 0.7 mile until the road ends.

10. Turn right onto State Road.

    The **Lake Tashmoo Overlook** appears immediately on the right. Pull over to observe a picture-postcard view of Lake Tashmoo and Vineyard Sound beyond. A century ago, a channel was dredged from Vineyard Sound to the lake so that ships could sail into this safe harbor. Before the dredging, annual dipping for herring in this freshwater pond was a popular springtime activity.

11. Take your next right onto Lambert's Cove Road.

    This narrow road twists, turns, ascends, and descends for 4.3 miles. Rolling farmland dotted with small ponds and bordered by stone walls and tall shade trees makes the effort worthwhile. The road curves around to Lambert's Cove, once a thriving fishing and farming community that had its own ferry running to Woods Hole. To explore **Ripley's Field Preserve** (mellow off-road biking, chapter 13), proceed 0.7 mile from the State Road intersection and turn left onto John Hoft Road.

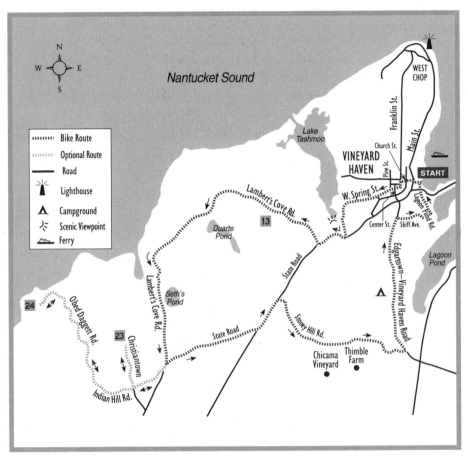

🚲WEST TISBURY NORTH LOOP

Duarte's Pond, one of the newer properties owned by the Martha's Vineyard Land Bank, lies 2 miles from State Road and 0.5 mile from the Tisbury–West Tisbury town line sign. The Land Bank is planning to cut trails around this tranquil pond.

Also on the left, just past the Tisbury–West Tisbury town line sign, are the remaining cultivated cranberry bogs on the island. Once there were many bogs on the Vineyard, but high transportation costs made it too difficult for growers to compete with cranberry producers on Cape Cod. The Vineyard Open Land Foundation is seeking funds to restore these old bogs.

If you are biking before Memorial Day, or after Labor Day, you can visit my favorite beach, Lambert's Cove. (During the summer only West Tisbury residents are allowed on the beach.) The parking lot sits next to the road, 1 mile from Duarte's Pond (3 miles from State Road). To see the cove, you must walk 0.25 mile down the path.

Just after the parking lot, on the right, sits a small, quaint white church. The Lambert's Cove Church has contained services here since 1846.

You won't miss **Seth's Pond**, located on the left 0.7 mile from Lambert's Cove Beach. You can see its small sandy beach from the road.

12. Lambert's Cove Road rejoins State Road. If you wish to extend your ride on Indian Hill Road and/or visit **Christiantown** and the **Mayhew Chapel** (chapter 23) and **Cedar Tree Neck Wildlife Sanctuary** (chapter 24), turn right on State Road.

    To extend your ride, take an immediate right onto Indian Hill Road. The long paved driveway on your left leads to Up-Island Cronig's and Biga Bakery, which sell food and drinks.

    If you are interested in seeing Mayhew Chapel or walking around Christiantown Woods, proceed 0.5 mile up Indian Hill Road and turn right onto Christiantown Road. The chapel lies 0.6 mile down this dirt road.

    To continue on to Cedar Tree Neck (beware, the mile-long entrance road is rutted, rocky, sandy, and quite steep), mount your bike and go back up the dirt road to Indian Hill Road. Turn right and climb the hill for about a mile, until you see a sign on the right for Cedar Tree Neck. Turn right onto the dirt road and follow the sanctuary signs for 1 mile.

    Don't let all the driveways confuse you. Continue straight on the road until it forks and then bear left. Mountain and hybrid bikes are more suited to this terrain, but all bikers should be wary on this road.

13. To return to Vineyard Haven from Lambert's Cove or Indian Hill Roads, turn left onto State Road.

14. Proceed 1.8 miles from Upper Lambert's Cove Road (0.5 mile from County Road) and turn right onto unpaved Stoney Hill Road, marked by signs advertising Chicama Vineyard and Thimble Farm. **Warning**: the road is often sandy and resembles a washboard.

Chicama Vineyard, located 1 mile down the road on the right, was the first vineyard since colonial days to plant European wine grapes. Every afternoon until 4:30 P.M., Chicama Vineyard offers free, forty-five-minute wine tours and tastings.

Thimble Farm is located on the right side of the road, less than half (0.3) a bumpy mile from Chicama Vineyard. At Thimble Farm you can pick your own strawberries or raspberries, depending on which berry is available. In back of the picking fields stands a large greenhouse, where tomatoes are grown year-round in a computer-controlled climate.

15. Continue on Stoney Hill Road (the last 0.5 mile is paved but has many speed bumps) until you come to the Edgartown–Vineyard Haven Road. Turn left onto the bike path toward Vineyard Haven.

16. After riding 1.4 miles, the bike path ends. Cross over to the right side of the road and pedal for 0.4 mile to Skiff Avenue. Turn right on Skiff, a great TAT—Traffic Avoidance Technique—to escape the congested junction with State Road. It's also an excellent way to end a ride: a steep downhill enhanced by views of Lagoon Pond.

17. Turn left at the end of the descent onto Lagoon Pond Road.

18. Lagoon Pond Road joins four other roads at the hazardous Five Corners intersection. Walk your bike across the road and continue on Water Street.

19. Water Street meets Union Street. You can either turn right toward the ferry dock or turn left toward Mad Martha's to reward yourself for all those hills you climbed.

CHAPTER SEVEN

Chilmark Loop

The Chilmark Loop offers a great workout, varied landscapes, and many exploratory options. This route highlights the dramatic physical differences between the island towns: from the rolling farmland of West Tisbury to the Vermont-like landscape of Chilmark. With its antique farmhouses, hilly tree-shaded roads, and rural character, Chilmark more closely resembles northern New England than an island resort community.

You can go for the workout and complete the trip in two to three hours, or opt for a leisurely day trip with possible stops at any of the six conservation areas and the quaint fishing village of Menemsha to swim, stroll, shop, and sightsee.

Distance: Round-trip from Edgartown, 34.5 miles.

Difficulty: Flat terrain until Middle Road in Chilmark, which is hilly; 28 miles of bike paths; no bike paths in West Tisbury and Chilmark.

Stops along the way: Priester's Pond Preserve, Waskosim's Rock Reservation, Great Rock Bight Preserve, Menemsha Hills Reservation, Menemsha, Fulling Mill Brook Preserve, Peaked Hill Reservation, Middle Road Sanctuary.

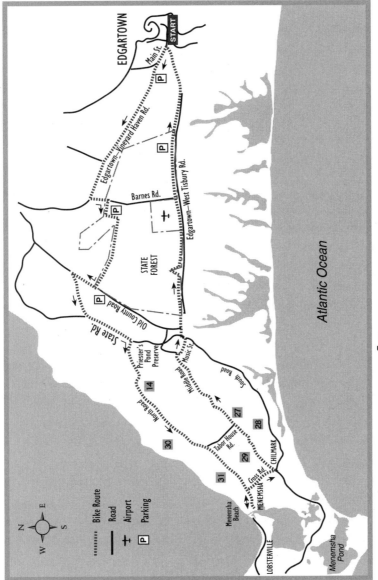

Food and drink: Edgartown, on Upper Main Street: the Fresh Pasta Shoppe, A & P supermarket; West Tisbury, on State Road: Up-Island Cronig's, the Vineyard Food Shop; on South Road: Alley's General Store; Menemsha, overlooking Menemsha Basin: Galley Snack Bar, Deli on Basin Road.

Restrooms: Edgartown: in the Visitor Center on Church Street, between Main Street and Pease's Point Way;

Menemsha: on the east side of the public parking lot for Menemsha Beach and Harbor.

THE ROUTE

Vineyard Haven bikers: Follow directions to Aquinnah (chapter 8) to the "blinker" and pick up the directions at No. 3.

Oak Bluff bikers: Follow the directions for the West Tisbury South Loop (chapter 5) to the "blinker" and pick up directions at No. 3.

1.   Begin the trip in Edgartown on the Main Street side of Cannonball Park, also known as Memorial Park.

     This triangular park, landscaped with cannons and balls from the Charlestown Navy Yard in Boston, memorializes the men who died in the Civil War. Proceed west on the bike path along Upper Main Street, past a wide variety of stores and restaurants conveniently located for stocking up on supplies before your trip.

     The Fresh Pasta Shoppe on your left makes excellent sandwiches and pizzas. On your right, the A & P supermarket has ready-made sandwiches and a salad bar.

2.   Continue straight at the fork onto the Edgartown–Vineyard Haven Road. Remain on this road for 4 miles until you reach the "blinker," the only traffic light on the island.

3.   Turn left (south) at the blinking yellow light onto the bike path on Barnes Road.

4.   Proceed 0.5 mile down Barnes Road and turn right onto the bike path that heads into the State Forest. The path travels west for 0.5 mile and turns south for another 0.5 mile.

5.   After completing the 0.5 mile south, keep your eyes open for an easy-to-miss path emerging from the right. Turn right and bike 2.2 more miles through the forest.

6.   Pedal past the barrier to Old County Road. Turn right.

7.   After pedaling 1 mile you'll reach State Road. Turn left and remain on this road for 2.6 miles, following the signs first to Aquinnah (Gay Head) and then to Menemsha.

After 1.5 miles you'll see Up-Island Cronig's market on the right, where you can stop for food or drink. Farther up the road, on the left, is the Vineyard Food Shop, known for its tasty pastries and breads.

8. At the junction of State and North Roads, bear right following the sign toward Menemsha.

On the far corner of the junction lies **Priester's Pond Preserve**, a small but special Land Bank property. Leave your bike in the rack at the North Road entrance and walk down the short path to Priester's Pond. The path forks; a left turn skirts the edge of the pond and crosses a tiny bridge with a waterfall below. A right turn leads to a log bench at the edge of the pond, where you can rest, reflect, and rejuvenate.

Up the road 1.5 mile you'll see the West Tisbury–Chilmark town line sign. Soon after on the left lies **Waskosim's Rock Reservation** (chapter 14), a great spot for off-road biking. If you are interested in swimming in an uncrowded bay, continue 2.2 miles to **Great Rock Bight Preserve** (chapter 30), located on the right, 0.5 mile down a dirt road. For hiking, continue on to **Menemsha Hills Reservation** (chapter 31), also on the right, 1 mile west of Great Rock Bight.

9. The first left, 0.5 mile after Menemsha Hills Reservation, is Menemsha Cross Road. To complete the Chilmark Loop, turn left, but if you wish to visit the tiny fishing village of Menemsha, continue straight on North Road.

The Wampanoag Indian translation for **Menemsha** is "place of observation," and indeed, this picturesque village is a great place to look around. Located in the town of Chilmark, Menemsha is bounded by Menemsha Pond, Menemsha Basin, and Vineyard Sound.

A right turn on Basin Road, the first street on the right after the steep downhill into Menemsha, leads to **Menemsha Beach**. Situated next to the harbor, this small public beach draws throngs of visitors who eagerly await and then applaud the striking sunset over the water.

To continue your tour of Menemsha, retrace your route on Basin Road and turn right, toward Menemsha Basin. The Galley, situated across from the basin on the right side of the road, prepares delicious lobster rolls, along with a variety of sandwiches and soft-serve ice cream.

Menemsha Basin provides a safe harbor for fishing vessels that unload bluefish, tuna, halibut, scrod, bass, swordfish, and lobster. The basin originally was a natural tidal creek that supplied an erratic flow of water into Menemsha Pond. In order to create this busy harbor, workers had to pile rocks at the entrance to the basin and repeatedly dredge the bottom.

Turn right to walk the length of **Dutcher Dock,** past the Coast Guard station, to note the nets, lobster pots, rigging, buoys, and shacks—a colorful testament to this active fishing community. If you look west across the channel, you'll discover **Lobsterville**, the most important fishing village on Martha's Vineyard one hundred years ago.

To continue your ride, return to the main road, ascend the steep grade, and turn right onto the Menemesha Cross Road.

10. Pedal 1 mile on the cross road.

   At **Beetlebung Corner** (also Chilmark Center, comprising the town hall, firehouse, and the Methodist Church), turn left onto Middle Road. "Beetlebung" is the island name for the tupelo tree. A cluster of tupelos grow on the south corner of Middle Road.

11. Remain on this hilly road for 4.3 miles.

   Middle Road is my personal favorite because it's shaded, uncrowded, and so picturesque. As I'm pumping up the hills, I enjoy watching the Tiasquam River flow by farms nestled near its banks. After each ascent I love being rewarded by a panoramic view of the Vineyard's south coast.

   Hiking opportunities abound along this road: **Fulling Mill Brook Preserve** (chapter 28) is located on the right, 1.3 miles from Beetlebung Corner. A back access road to **Peaked Hill Reservation** (chapter 29) is located almost directly across Middle Road from the preserve. **Middle Road Sanctuary** (chapter 27) sits on the right, 0.5 mile from Fulling Mill Brook.

12. At the T intersection with Music Street, turn right toward the center of West Tisbury, a town that continues to reflect its origins as a rural farming village.

13. Turn left at the junction with South Road.

If you need refreshment, ahead on the left lies the inviting porch of **Alley's General Store.** Upon entering Alley's, whose sign boasts "Dealers in Almost Everything," one is transported a hundred years back to the pre-supermarket era, when the general store supplied provisions and was the center of a community's social life.

Back Alley's, at the rear of the parking lot, is a cafe that sells take-out food. Across the street lies the **Field Gallery,** where delightful sculptures by Tom Maley scamper over the grounds.

14.   At the fork keep to the right, remaining on the Edgartown–West Tisbury Road for the 9-mile return to Edgartown.

Almost immediately, on your left, is the picturesque Mill Pond, often surrounded by ducks and swans patiently waiting for generous travelers to stop and feed them.

15.   The bike path begins 0.5 mile farther on the left side of the road, behind Hostelling International, which provides rooms and cooking facilities for cyclists. To gain access to the path, cut across the playing field adjacent to the hostel. The path lies directly behind the field.

16.   Go right, in an easterly direction, on the path. This scenic but hilly route winds its way through the forest. Although the path is generally straight, it takes an abrupt turn into the forest in order to bypass a wedge of privately owned land.

17.   Continue east, passing the airport and crossing Barnes Road. At this point bikers returning to Oak Bluffs or Vineyard Haven should turn left on Barnes Road and ride 2.4 miles to the "blinker." Edgartown cyclists should remain on the Edgartown–West Tisbury Road.

18.   Proceed 1.7 miles to the end of the old bike path and bear left onto the newer section.

19.   Pedal 0.1 mile and cross the Edgartown–West Tisbury Road to continue on the bike path for 2.3 miles.

Morning Glory Farm lies on the right, 1.5 miles after the road crossing.

20.   After the bike path ends, remain on the Edgartown–West Tisbury Road for 0.3 mile to Cannonball Park.

CHAPTER EIGHT

Aquinnah (Gay Head) and Lobsterville Loop

The trip from Vineyard Haven to Aquinnah and back, spanning 21 miles in each direction, is the most strenuous but also the most rewarding ride in this book.

> *The rolling terrain creates the strain,*
> *But don't complain; there is much to gain*
> *From the scenery, which, in the main,*
> *Does, indeed, lessen the pain!*

In order to reach Aquinnah you must bike through Chilmark, whose rolling hills and landscape resemble northern New England. When you reach remote Aquinnah, you will discover that it is very different from other island towns. Many Wampanoags have settled in Aquinnah, one of two Native American townships in Massachusetts, and the town reflects this heritage. Most of the Wampanoag tribe no longer earn their living farming and fishing, as did their ancestors. Some are now store proprietors selling Native American crafts and memorabilia in the shops on top of the Aquinnah Cliffs.

Additional rewards for climbing these rolling hills are relaxing on Aquinnah Beach, viewing the colorful cliffs from below, and then ascending to the top for the panorama that's drawing all those tour buses (see chapter 32).

Distance: 42 miles round-trip from the ferry terminal in Vineyard Haven; add 3 miles to visit Lobsterville.

Difficulty: Strenuous.

Stops along the way: Nashaquitsa Overlook, Aquinnah Cliffs and Beach.

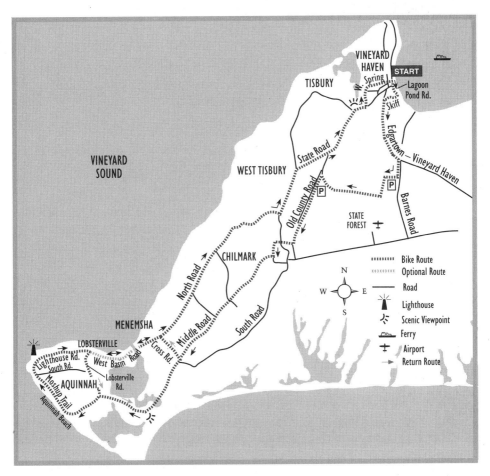

🚲 AQUINNAH & LOBSTERVILLE LOOP

Food and drink: Vineyard Haven: A & P supermarket, Black Dog Bakery; Chilmark: Chilmark Chocolates, Chilmark Store; Aquinnah: shops near top of cliffs; West Tisbury: Vineyard Food Shop, Cronig's Down-Island Market, Biga Bakery.

Restrooms: Vineyard Haven: in the Steamship Authority terminal on Union Street;
Aquinnah: portable toilets at the entrance to the beach and in a small building adjacent to the parking lot (there is a fee).

THE ROUTE

Edgartown bikers: Go west on the Edgartown–Vineyard Haven Road to the "blinker" at Barnes Road. Turn left and pick up these directions at No. 6.
Oak Bluff bikers: Follow the directions in the West Tisbury South Loop in chapter 5 through direction No. 6, and then continue on the Edgartown–Vineyard Haven Road to the blinker at Barnes Road. Turn left and pick up the directions in this chapter at No. 6.

1. From the Steamship Authority terminal in Vineyard Haven, walk your bike through the traffic up Union Street to Water Street, the first road on the left.

2. Turn left on Water Street.
    The Black Dog Bakery on the left side of Water Street sells delicious breads and pastries in addition to sandwiches and soups. On the right side, the A & P sells typical supermarket fare, along with decent prepared food at their deli counter.

3. At the Five Corners intersection walk your bike straight across State Road to Lagoon Pond Road.

4. Take the first right onto Skiff Avenue and ascend the hill (training for higher, longer hills ahead!).

5. Follow Skiff to the T intersection with the Edgartown–Vineyard Haven Road. Turn left. Pedal 0.4 mile to the bike path.

6. Continue on the bike path for 1.7 miles until you reach the blinker, the only traffic light on the island. Turn right at the blinker onto the bike path on the right side of Barnes Road.

7. Pedal 0.5 mile in the direction of the airport. Turn right onto the bike path heading into the Manuel F. Correllus State Forest. The path heads west for 0.5 mile and then veers sharply south for another 0.5 mile.

8. *Don't miss* the right turn onto a bike path that leads to West Tisbury. This path cuts through the forest for 2 miles.

9. Turn left before the barrier, which prevents vehicles other than bikes from using the path, onto a path that emerges from the left.

10. Bike for 1 mile until the path no longer parallels County Road and begins to veer south. Bear right onto the side path to County Road. Continue biking south on County Road.

11. Remain on County Road for 1 mile. Upon reaching the Granary Gallery on your left, a popular art gallery which carries pictures by island artists and photographers, turn right onto Scotchmans Lane (you may not find a street sign, which is typical of the island's rural areas).

12. Stay on this road for 0.7 mile, crossing the intersection with State Road and then passing the Agricultural Society Hall and Grounds, site of the annual agricultural fair. After riding by a fenced wildlife refuge on your right, turn right onto the first paved street, Middle Road. Again, there may not be a street sign.

13. Remain on scenic Middle Road, ascending and descending for 4.3 miles until you reach Chilmark Center at the junction of Middle, Menemsha Cross, and South Roads. Go straight through the intersection onto South Road toward Aquinnah.

    Tupelo

    The name of this intersection, Beetlebung Corner, describes how the first English settlers used the wood from the **tupelo trees**, which grow in the left corner of Middle Road. They formed the tupelo's tough, dense wood into "beetles," or wooden mallets, and "bungs," or corks for plugging the holes in barrels. The colonists then used the "beetles" to hammer "bungs" into barrels.

    If you need to refill your water bottle, you'll find a hose to the right of the Chilmark Store, located on the right side of South Road just past Beetlebung Corner. This shop sells a variety of food-stuffs but specializes in delicious pizza and iced coffee drinks.

    But if you really want an energy boost, head for Chilmark Chocolates, my favorite candy store, just down the road on the right. When you enter the shop you will be dazzled by the array of confections, but don't forget to look through the window on your right to watch the candy-making process, which is performed by people with disabilities. You can quench your thirst at the water faucet to the right of the deck. Biking the many miles to Aquinnah (Gay Head) ensures a guilt-free stop at this unique establishment.

14. Remain on this arduous but scenic stretch of road for 3.5 miles.

One mile from Chilmark Chocolates is **Nashaquitsa Overlook**, a turnoff that offers a spectacular view of Nashaquitsa Pond, which flows into Menemsha Pond (chapter 43). Look to the right for the fishing village of Menemsha, nestled next to the ocean. If you are blessed with a clear day, you can peer out across the water to the Elizabeth Islands, perched between Vineyard Sound and Buzzards Bay.

One mile after the scenic turnout, between a downhill run and a steep uphill, on the left side of the road stands a pipe from an artesian well that supplies cold, tasty water to thirsty cyclists.

15. Turn left onto Moshup Trail. Follow Moshup Trail for 3 miles to the public beach on the left. If you wish to stop to swim or walk near the ocean, head down the boardwalk and park your bike in the rack on the beach.

16. To continue the ride, head up the road to the lighthouse and cliffs, the destination of all the tour buses that have whizzed by. A bike rack is located next to the parking lot. See chapter 32 for information on the beach and Aquinnah Cliffs.

17. The return trip cuts across the north side of the island to the Lobsterville section of Aquinnah. From the cliffs, pedal back toward the parking lot, and turn left onto Lighthouse Road. This 2-mile stretch parallels South Road, offering panoramic views of Dogfish Bay.

One hundred years ago, before the creation of Menemsha Harbor, **Lobsterville** was the most important fishing village on Martha's Vineyard. Ships from New York made daily visits to purchase fish and lobster. Now the village no longer exists and the area is used for beaching, fishing, and enjoying the views of Menemsha Harbor and Menemsha Pond.

You can choose to take an optional 3-mile side visit or bike ferry trip to Menemsha. Continue past the junction with Lobsterville Road and proceed for another 1.5 mile, passing through Lobsterville to Menemsha Basin. From there you can take the bike ferry to Menemsha (a steep fee, but it eliminates 6.8 miles) and pick up the directions at No. 22, or you can turn around, return on the same road, and continue to follow the directions.

On the way to this former harbor, you pass **Lobsterville Beach**, part of the Aquinnah Reserve and open to the public. If you want to stop and swim, wheel your bike onto the beach and jump in.

The Cranberry Lands, across from the beach, are covered with wild roses, bayberry bushes, and cranberries.

The road ends at Memesha Basin. Across the channel sits the village of Menemsha, a thriving fishing port and home to many of the vessels whose owners continue to earn their living from the sea. If you look north across Vineyard Sound you'll see Naushon, the largest Elizabeth Island.

18. To return to South Road, retrace your route on West Basin Road until you reach Lobsterville Road. Turn left onto Lobsterville Road and climb for 0.7 mile.

19. At the intersection with South Road, turn left and proceed 4.9 miles to Beetlebung Corner. The first right turn on South Road leads to the new Wampanoag Tribal Office.

20. At Beetlebung Corner, turn left on Menemsha Cross Road, heading toward Menemsha.

21. At the junction with North Road turn right, following the signs to Vineyard Haven. Remain on this road for 10 miles until you reach West Spring Street in Vineyard Haven.

North Road is my preferred return route: It's flatter, and its many commercial establishments provide good excuses to stop.

22. Turn left onto West Spring Street, the next street after the Lake Tashmoo Overlook.

23. Follow West Spring as it bends around. Bear left at the fork and then bend right, keeping the school on the right. Remain on Spring, which runs into Main Street in Vineyard Haven Center.

24. Turn left on Main.

25. Turn right onto Union Street, which returns to the Steamship Authority Wharf.

CHAPTER NINE

Manuel F. Corellus State Forest—East

This 4,343-acre state forest offers endless opportunities for off-road biking—from wide sandy fire lanes to overgrown, twisty, deep old cart paths. For cyclists accustomed to mainland biking, the challenge here is plowing through sand. (clue: shift into low gear and spin your wheels). I have designed two State Forest loops—one east of the airport, and the other west, with a great connector between the two. This eastern loop chapter includes a bridle path, fire lane, and a section of the Dr. Fisher Road, a path created more than 150 years ago by a wealthy Edgartown resident to carry grain from his gristmill in West Tisbury to Edgartown.

Directions to connect with the western loop are included at the end of this chapter.

Because some of the single-track trails are often overgrown, wear long pants tucked into socks, and long sleeves to protect from shrub scratches, ticks, and poison ivy.

Directions: From Vineyard Haven follow the Edgartown–Vineyard Haven Road for 2.7 miles to Martha's Vineyard Regional High School. Turn right onto Sanderson Avenue, just to the left (east) of the school. Follow Sanderson for 1 mile. The route begins on the left, behind the fire road barrier gate (at the

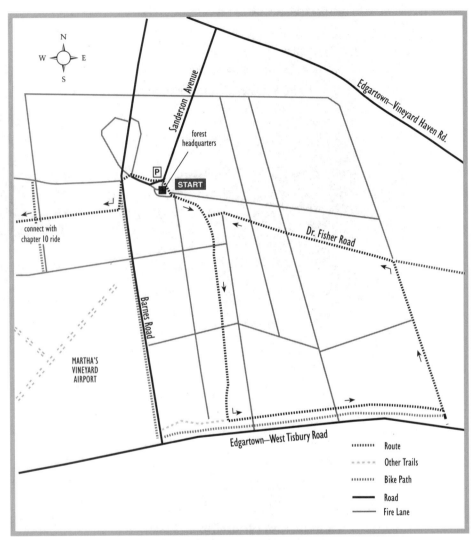

STATE FOREST EAST

point where the road turns right). The forest supervisor office is ahead. You can park your car on the side of the road.

Distance: 4.6 miles; connector trail to western loop is 2.2 miles.

Difficulty: Easy, flat, mostly single-track, often overgrown, with 0.5 mile on a wide fire road.

Background: In 1908 the commonwealth of Massachusetts paid $1 plus back taxes for 612 acres of centrally located land to use as a sanctuary for the endangered heath hen. However, the heath hen did not fare any better on the Vineyard than anywhere else. None has been seen in the forest for more than sixty years. In 1925 the state began to buy much of the surrounding land. Within two years the forest had grown to its present 4,343 acres.

Due to frequent fires, which retarded tree growth, the forest remained a sandplain grassland habitat until 1934. At that time the Civilian Conservation Corps planted **red pine**, **white pine**, and **spruce** trees. Unfortunately, many red pines, which thrive in colder northern regions, adjusted poorly to the

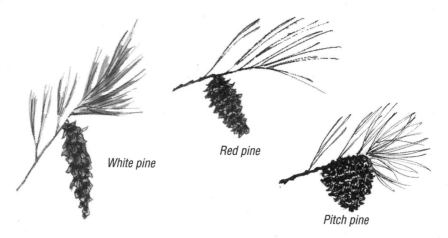

White pine

Red pine

Pitch pine

Vineyard's more temperate climate. The red pines became stressed and fell prey to disease, primarily the fungus *Diplodea pinea*. As you bike through the forest you will see dead tree trunks, remnants of this species of pine. The white pine and spruce trees are better adapted to this climate and continue to thrive.

Manuel F. Corellus began working in the forest in 1938. He became supervisor ten years later and remained in that position until 1987. In 1988, in recognition of his fifty years of dedication to the forest, it was named in his honor.

THE ROUTE

1. Turn left and pedal past the gate onto the fire road.
2. Take the second left onto a narrow dirt road.

3. Remain on the road as it bears right into a meadow and passes a stand of white spruce trees. After crossing a fire lane, the trail starts out wide and grassy but gradually narrows to a single-track path.

4. Continue on this trail, which proceeds in a southerly direction, for 1 mile. Keep your eye out for an intersection with a narrow trail. Turn left. (If you reach the paved bike path, you've gone too far.)

    This trail begins as a "half-track" and then widens as it heads east, running parallel to the paved bike path for 1.3 miles. Upon entering a pine forest, you may lose the path. Look for occasional red blazes on pine trees. Be prepared to jump logs and maneuver around tree roots and poison ivy. (If you do rub up against poison ivy, scrub the area with soap upon your return.)

5. The trail ends at a fire road lined with telephone poles. Turn left. You can ride the 0.5 mile on the sandy road or pedal on the narrow path to the right of the fire lane.

    A paved bike path may replace the narrow path. The Martha's Vineyard Commission is seeking state funds to build a paved connector path to the western half of the forest.

    If you are traveling in midsummer, look on the left side of the fire lane for **lowbush blueberry** bushes. Interspersed with the blueberries are clumps of small yellow flowers named **wild indigo**. This plant's name is derived from the blue dye produced by soaking its leaves in water.

6. After crossing a fire road and passing a telephone pole, watch on your left for a single-track trail emerging from the woods. Turn left onto the old Dr. Fisher Road. (The path also continues to the right, and, at last visit, there was a Dr. Fisher Road sign.)

    You can tell the path's age and amount of use by how much lower it is than the surrounding terrain. One hundred fifty years ago this road was a main thoroughfare between North Tisbury and Edgartown. When I last rode the Dr. Fisher Road, it was significantly wider and easier to negotiate than the single track on the first half of the loop.

7. Remain on the trail for 1.4 miles, until it empties into a fire lane. Bear right and proceed straight on the dirt road to retrace your route to the starting point.

TO EXTEND YOUR RIDE AND CONNECT WITH THE FOREST WEST LOOP:

8. From the dirt road pass through the barrier gate, pedal by Sanderson Avenue, and continue straight down the paved road.

9. At the intersection with Barnes Road, cross the road and follow the path. Once on the paved bike path, turn left.

10. Proceed 0.25 mile and turn right after passing one yellow steel post and before reaching the second one. The turnoff is located in an open section of the forest at the point where the gray cedar stakes meet the gray cedar fence, to the left of the brown barrier gate with red stripes. The trail begins as a wide grassy trail and then narrows to a single track.

11. After pedaling about 0.2 mile, bear left at the fork (easy turn to miss; the right fork leads to a fire road).

12. Continue as the trail winds through a pine forest to the paved bike path. Turn right onto the bike path.

13. Watch for an opening in the brush and take a quick left onto a dirt path. Remain on the path as it winds through the forest.

14. Upon reaching the fire road, turn left. I suggest riding on the grassy strip to the right of the sandy fire lane. Remain on the road through two intersections with fire lanes. Martha's Vineyard Airport will be on your left.

15. Turn right at the second fire lane intersection and follow the Forest West Loop directions starting at No. 5.

CHAPTER TEN

Manuel F. Corellus State Forest—West

This 5-mile tour of the western side of the forest winds through woodlands on a variety of terrain, from pine-needle-covered, twisty, single-tracks to ankle-deep half-tracks. Wide, sandy fire roads, designed to provide access to the forest's 4,343 acres, crisscross the land and offer periodic opportunities to bail out.

To connect with Forest East Loop, follow the directions from No. 5.

Directions: This route begins in the forest, just off the Edgartown–West Tisbury Road, 2.2 miles west of Barnes Road, 1.6 miles west of the airport entrance road and directly across from Pond Road; parking for three cars is adjacent to the paved bike path.

Distance: 5 miles; add 2.2 miles to connect with the Forest East Loop.

Difficulty: Moderate; mostly flat with a few short hills. Trails can be narrow and deep or wide and sandy; oak saplings often encroach on the trail. Wear long pants and sleeves for protection.

THE ROUTE

1. Begin on the paved bike path as it heads into the forest. (At this point the bike path stops paralleling the Edgartown–West Tisbury Road and veers sharply north to avoid a wedge of private land on the left.)

2. Pedal approximately 500 feet. Turn right onto a narrow path.

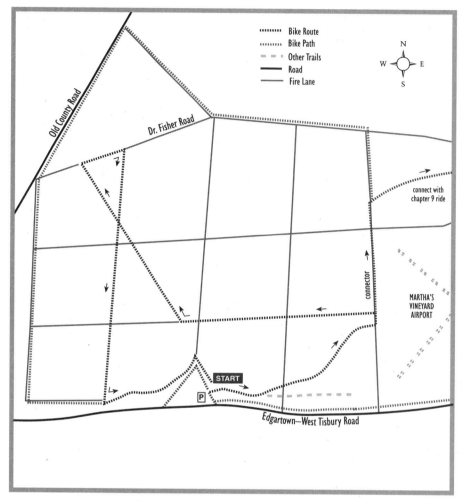

Legend:
- Bike Route
- Bike Path
- Other Trails
- Road
- Fire Lane

Old County Road

Dr. Fisher Road

connect with chapter 9 ride

connector

MARTHA'S VINEYARD AIRPORT

START

P

Edgartown—West Tisbury Road

STATE FOREST WEST

3. Remain on the path for 0.3 mile and look closely on your left for a narrow path. Turn left.

Have fun on this pine-needle-covered trail that twists and turns through the forest. The major obstacles are tree trunks lining the path, which don't provide quite enough clearance for wide handlebars.

Soon the trail crosses a fire lane and enters a frost bottom, a low, sandy area created by glacial melting. When the last ice sheet began to melt and recede more than fifteen thousand years ago, it dropped millions of tons of sand that it had picked up during its slow southern flow. Much of the Vineyard was formed from the runoff of this sandy residue.

The glacier carved away this lower elevation, which can be considerably hotter or colder than the surrounding terrain. As a result, it experiences earlier and later frosts than the higher ground. Only certain species can live in a microclimate with temperature drops that destroy early spring growth. The hardy **scrub oak** is one type of plant that manages to survive under these conditions, but it grows much smaller than normal.

After pedaling 0.2 mile along the frost bottom, the path becomes very sandy and difficult to negotiate. Be prepared to dismount. Fortunately the trail ascends and enters a pine forest. At this point, it may be hard to detect a trail, but look to your left for the continuation of a sandy path.

Lichen grows on both sides of the trail. Lichen is a grayish green flowerless plant composed of an alga and fungus living together as a single unit. Each contributes to the whole: the alga supplying food; the fungus, water. Lichens are very sensitive to sulfur dioxide, a polluting gas. If lichen grows in an area, its presence indicates that the air is not polluted. So during your ride, go for it, and gulp top-quality air.

4. The trail ends at a fire lane bordering the airport's runway. Turn left.

5. Make a quick left onto another fire lane. To continue the Forest West Loop, ignore the following directions and go directly to No. 6. But to connect with the Forest East Loop, do **not** turn left.

Connector Option: Instead, proceed straight, passing two fire-lane intersections. After the second intersection, go 300 feet and turn right onto a dirt path that heads into the forest. At the intersection with the bike path, turn right and then make a quick left onto another dirt path. Continue straight as a path heads off to the left. Upon reaching the bike path that runs next to Barnes (Airport) Road, turn left. Turn right onto a dirt path that leads into Barnes Road. Cross the road and follow the paved road up the hill toward the state forest headquarters. At the intersection with Sanderson Avenue go straight, crossing a barrier onto a fire road. Pick up the directions for the Forest East Loop.

6. Pedal straight, through intersections with two fire lanes. The first section of fire lane is easy riding; the second is sandier and trickier to navigate.

    After the intersection with the second fire lane, continue straight, heading up an incline. Go about 600 feet to a single-track trail that intersects the fire road. Turn right (a little grass island separates two entrances to the trail).

    The challenge here is to keep your wheel straight on this narrow, deep path that runs first through an oak woodland and then through another sandy frost bottom covered with scrub oaks. Without the benefit of pine needles or leaves to cover the trail, the island's sandplain origins become most apparent. The trail enters a pine forest dotted with roots. The trail widens as it leaves the forest, and crosses a fire road.

7. Follow the dirt path into another pine forest.

8. Cross another fire lane. This deep section of path requires plenty of concentration.

9. The trail ends at the third fire lane. Turn right.

10. At the intersection with the next fire lane, turn right onto this grassy area that resembles a double-track more than a fire road. This road intersects with the single-track you just rode. You can turn left and return on that same route, or remain on the fire lane for 1 mile to the junction with another single-track trail.

11. If you choose to remain on the fire lane, you'll soon discover that the grass turns to sand and then mixes with rocks.

    It's interesting to observe what persistently has sprouted despite frequent cuttings along the fire roads. Pine seedlings, blueberry and huckleberry bushes, heather, sweet fern—a low-growing shrub whose branches look like a fern—wild indigo, and a variety of ground covers, including bearberry.

12. After pedaling for 1 mile on the fire road, and just before you reach the paved bike path, turn left onto a single-track trail. (There may be a sign attached to a tree announcing the trail.) All the energy you conserved biking on the fire road can be expended on heading up the steep incline into the forest. (Pine tree roots add to the challenge.)

13. After a steep, gravelly descent, turn left either onto the paved bike path or onto the single-track that borders the pavement.

14. Proceed to the junction where the paved bike path abruptly turns and heads south. Follow the path back to your starting point.

CHAPTER ELEVEN

Brine's Pond—Chappy Five Corners Preserves

Brine's Pond and Chappy Five Corners Preserves are protected conservation areas owned by the Martha's Vineyard Land Bank Commission. Both are located on Chappaquiddick and are only 0.5 mile apart, but they offer two very different experiences. The central focus of Brine's Pond Preserve is an island of beetlebung trees perched in the center of a freshwater pond, while the Chappy Five Corners Preserve exhibits a colorful wetland sitting in the middle of a dense forest. Both properties support an abundance of blueberry and huckleberry bushes to fortify hungry hikers and bikers.

The Land Bank has stated that the trails in both preserves will be expanded and made handicapped accessible. The connecting route between the two properties may change, so check the trail map boards when entering each area.

Directions: From the ferry that runs continually between Edgartown and Chappaquiddick, follow the main road for 1.6 miles. Brine's Pond Preserve sits on the right side of the road, just past the Chappaquiddick Community Center. If coming by automobile, you can park in the lot behind the community center.

Distance: 3 miles—1 mile through Brine's Pond Preserve, 0.5 mile around Chappy Five Corners Preserve, 0.6 mile on the dirt road connecting the two.

Difficulty: Easy.

Restrooms: Chappaquiddick Community Center.

Food and drink: Chappy General Store, on Chappaquiddick Road, 0.5 mile past Brine's Pond.

Background: Both preserves are good examples of fallow-field succession, where certain varieties of plants are replaced by others over time. After a number of years of this gradual replacement, the entire community is changed. During the eighteenth and nineteenth centuries, this area was mainly grassland and was used as pasture for sheep and cattle. When the settlers turned from farming to whaling, the ungrazed land was receptive to a variety of small shrubs such as huckleberry, blueberry, and bayberry, along with red cedar trees. When pitch pine trees succeeded the red cedars, they created enough shade for oak trees to get a foothold. The woods in both preserves are filled with pine trees growing among white and black oak trees. Most Vineyard forests are at this same stage of succession.

THE ROUTE

Brine's Pond Preserve

1. If starting from the parking lot of the Chappaquiddick Community Center, head toward the building and turn right onto the trail. If arriving on bike, enter from Chappaquiddick Road and head toward Brine's Pond.

2. Facing Brine's Pond, begin your exploration on the left (east) side of the pond.

    A close inspection of Brine's Pond reveals an island populated by a grove of beetlebung trees. Beetlebung is the Vineyard name for the **tupelo** tree. Early settlers used its dense wood for wooden "beetles" (mallets) which drove the "bungs" (corks) that were used to plug barrel holes.

3. Keeping Brine's Pond on your right, follow the trail until it meets the Red Trail. Turn left, following the Red Trail into the pine grove, where you will find sweet, mellow biking on wide trails covered with pine needles.

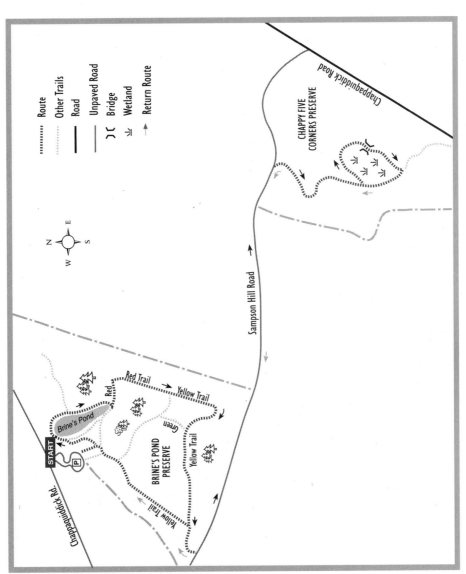

4. Bear right at the fork and take another quick right, remaining on the Red Trail.

5. At the fork leave the Red Trail and bear left onto the Yellow Trail.

   If you seek a tasty addition to your outdoor exploration, be alert for **blueberry** and **huckleberry** bushes, which often grow beneath oak trees. Both plants have small oval leaves, with huckleberry leaves typically darker and shinier. Both produce small bell-shaped flowers that become round berries in the summer. Huckleberries are usually a deep, dark blue and contain a tiny seed in the center. Blueberries are lighter, with a frosty cast.

   Be aware of the ubiquitous **poison ivy**. In its usual form it has shiny pointed leaves growing in clusters of three. It can inch along the ground or climb trees like a vine. If you discover poison ivy lurking between you and the berries, forget the berries. Otherwise you may go home with a very itchy souvenir.

6. Take the next right, remaining on the Yellow Trail. (Look for a yellow blaze on a tree to your left.)

7. At the junction with the Green Trail bear left, continuing on the Yellow Trail.

8. If you wish to explore Chappy Five Corners Preserve, leave the Yellow Trail and bear left onto the path that leads to Sampson Hill. (At 92 feet, it's the highest point on Chappaquiddick.) You may have to walk

Brine's Pond provides a scenic rest stop along this gentle off-road bike tour.

your bike, as the path is often narrow and overgrown. According to the Land Bank, this connector path may change.

9. The path runs by a house on the left. At the dirt road, turn left, passing the front of the same house.

10. Remain on the dirt road (Sampson Hill Road) for 0.2 mile. After 0.1 mile, on your right you will pass a fork in the road with a sign that points to Brine's Pond Preserve. On the left at 0.2 mile sits a gated driveway posted with the number 36. Across from the driveway is the new entrance to Chappy Five Corners Preserve. Turn right onto the path.

    If you continue on Sampson Hill Road for 0.5 mile, you'll reach Chappaquiddick Road. (The main entrance to Chappy Five Corners will be on the right.)

Chappy Five Corners Preserve

11. Bear right on the trail to pass an old homestead (a loop around the homestead may now be in place).

12. Bear right onto a carriage road to proceed into the preserve.

13. At the next junction turn left to head into the wetland.

    After cycling about 0.2 mile, and just after a short downhill, you will pedal over a tiny bridge constructed of wooden planks. Stop to look around at the type of plants that thrive in this moist environment. In the spring it's easy to spot dainty white flowers on the flowering **dogwood** trees. In the fall the bright-colored leaves on the maple and beetlebung trees are most apparent. **Greenbrier** is the name of the vine with many tendrils that is attaching itself to anything in its path.

14. After completing the loop you can turn right to head back toward Brine's Pond Preserve or turn left to go out the main entrance of Chappy Five Corners and continue your off-road riding at Poucha Pond Preserve (chapter 12), 0.5 mile up Wasque Road.

15. To return to Brine's Pond, turn right and follow the path to Sampson Hill Road.

16. Turn left onto the dirt road and pedal for 0.2 mile back to the narrow path.

17. Turn right onto the path.

18. At the junction with the Yellow Trail, turn left.

19. Remain on the Yellow Trail through the woods to return to the parking lot and the main entrance to Brine's Pond Preserve.

CHAPTER TWELVE

Poucha Pond Reservation

While biking around Chappaquiddick, stop at Poucha Pond Reservation for some mellow off-road riding on pine-needle-covered trails that wind through open fields and woods. The trail becomes muddy as you cycle along a salt marsh to small islands in Poucha Pond, a body of water that extends from famous Dike Bridge to remote Wasque Point. This marshy pond doesn't appeal to bathers but is favored by by kayakers who like to observe the many species of birds that feast on the abundant fin- and shellfish there.

Take along mosquito repellent. To swim, head for Wasque Reservation or East Beach.

Directions: The reservation is 3.8 miles from the Chappaquiddick ferry. Follow Chappaquiddick Road to Wasque Road and turn left. Proceed 0.5 mile to the entrance on the left side of the road.

Distance: 1.7 miles.

Restrooms: Located at Mytoi, East Beach (chapter 19), and Wasque Reservation (chapter 20).

Food and drink: Chappy General Store, located 2.2 miles from the ferry landing and 1.6 miles from the reservation.

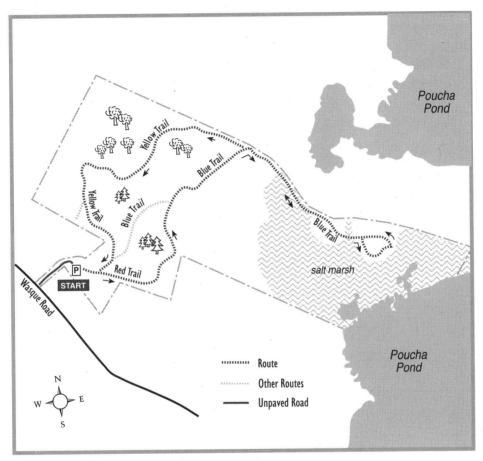

Poucha Pond

Poucha
Pond

salt marsh

Poucha
Pond

·········· Route

············ Other Routes

——— Unpaved Road

N
W —⊕— E
S

🚲POUCHA POND RESERVATION

Fees: Chappaquiddick ferry. At the time of publication, bikers pay $3 for a round-trip ride and drivers pay $5.

Background: During the last three hundred years the island's early settlers found many uses for this remote property. At one time Poucha Pond was open to the sea. Boats traveling near Martha's Vineyard's eastern shore used it as a harbor, but by 1722 storms and tides had filled the opening with sand.

In 1845 a few landowners constructed a dike in order to control the flow of water in and out of the pond. Each winter they closed the dike's gates to prevent salt water from entering. In the spring they opened the gates so the herring and shad could swim into the pond and deposit their eggs. Fishermen then caught the fish, which they pickled, salted, and shipped in barrels to New York.

During the nineteenth century the marsh also was put to good use. Farmers drove their livestock to graze on the nutritious marsh grass. As many as four barrels of wild cranberries per day were harvested from this bountiful wetland. Hunters were drawn to the marsh and pond because of the numerous migrating waterfowl that stopped to feed.

Now the pond is seeded, and thus produces scallops and clams which attract such shorebirds as terns, oystercatchers, and several varieties of gulls.

THE ROUTE

1. Proceed down the sandy entrance road to the parking lot and head down the path.

2. Fork right onto the Red Trail.

   While traveling through this typical Vineyard **pitch pine** forest, notice the small pine trees growing beside the trail. Whenever land is cleared, the cut pines quickly reappear because their large root systems lie close to the surface, waiting for enough open space to sprout.

   After leaving the pine forest, the path winds through a woodland filled with oak trees. Years ago this section was probably inhabited by pine trees. However, once the oak trees took hold, they overshadowed the pines, causing them to weaken and die. This process of succession often reveals how many years have elapsed since the land was farmed. The type of vegetation indicates each stage in the process: red cedar trees are often the first to sprout in open fields, followed by woody shrubs like huckleberry and blueberry. Pitch pine trees follow, and the last variety of tree in the order of succession is the oak.

   As you cycle towards the water, you will see more gnarled and deformed trees, victims of the strong winds that bombard this side of the island.

3. At the junction with the Blue Trail, bear right and follow the Blue Trail to the salt marsh.

   You'll find the **groundsel tree**, also called the high-tide bush, growing at the edge of the marsh. It's easier to spot this shrub in

Constant wind has stunted the growth of this scrub oak. Be sure to respect all property that is posted No Trespassing.

autumn, when the seeds on the female plant mature into small, white, feathery clusters.

This trail leads to several pond and marsh lookouts, excellent vantage points from which to spot **common** and **least terns** fishing the shallow water for minnows. You may also see great **black-backed** and **herring gulls**, which are responsible for the broken shells you see on the ground. The gulls pull the shellfish out of the water, fly into the air, and drop the shellfish to the hard ground. The gulls then swoop down and yank the contents out of the broken shells.

Three varieties of herons feed in the marsh: the **short green heron**, the **great blue heron**, and the **black-crowned night heron**. You may also spot **marsh hawks**, **egrets**, and **short-eared owls**.

These birds are drawn to the salt marsh to feed on finfish and shellfish that thrive in this nutrient-rich environment. An acre of salt marsh yields an estimated 242 pounds of nutrients, mostly in the form of vegetation, which in turn feeds about 300 pounds of shell-fish. Tides carry nutritious organic matter from the salt marsh into ponds and out to the ocean, where other species of fish feed on it.

4. Follow the trail as it goes through the salt marsh.

5. Bear right to take the loop that skirts the salt marsh.

6. After completing the loop, turn left to retrace your route on the Blue Trail through the marsh.

If you are biking or hiking in late summer or early fall, you will see the marsh ornamented with tiny purple flowers. This small, delicate plant is called **sea lavender**. Another fall flower is **seaside goldenrod**, which produces bright yellow flowers that line the edge of the marsh. The narrow channels you see cutting through the marsh are for mosquito control.

Two varieties of grasses growing here are **cordgrass** and **saltmarsh hay**. Cordgrass is the pioneer plant of salt marshes. It starts to grow at the edges of bays or ponds, where it produces stiff, broad leaves which die back at the end of each growing season. The yearly dying back yields the buildup of sediments necessary to support other plant species such as saltmarsh hay, a thinner, floppier grass. This hay is so rich in nutrients that the island's early settlers shepherded their livestock all the way to this remote corner so their animals could graze.

7. Remain on the Blue Trail until the intersection with the Yellow Trail. Bear right onto the Yellow Trail, lined with more wind-battered oak trees.

8. Bear left on the Yellow Trail as it merges with an old cart path and passes Wasque Farm on the right. Remain on the Yellow Trail as the cart path bears right.

9. At the intersection with the Blue Trail, turn right to return to the parking lot.

CHAPTER THIRTEEN

Tisbury Meadow—Wompesket— Ripley's Field Preserves

These three properties are linked by dirt roads, so cyclists can explore them all in one visit while their nonbiking companions can hike the trails in Tisbury Meadow. Tisbury Meadow and Ripley's Field boast wide, well-maintained trails through meadows and woodlands. Birdhouses dot the meadows, where eastern bluebirds, mockingbirds, tree swallows, chipping sparrows, northern orioles, and prairie warblers flit above wildflowers. Wompesket, the smallest and most rustic of the three properties, offers the most diverse landscape, consisting of wetlands, ponds, woods, and a large meadow.

Directions: Tisbury Meadow Preserve is located on State Road, 1.8 miles from the Steamship Authority terminal in Vineyard Haven and 0.4 mile past the Lake Tashmoo Overlook. After you pass Lambert's Cove Road on your right, look to your left for a driveway leading to a house and the sign for Tisbury Meadow Preserve.

Distance: 6.2 miles.

Difficulty: Easy to moderate; a few hills in Tisbury Meadow can pump up your pulse rate, but the trails in Wompesket offer the most challenge.

Food and drink: Cronig's Market on State Road in Tisbury sells groceries. West of Cronig's, at 157 State Road, Black Dog Bakery-Cafe sells pastry and sandwiches.

Background: All three properties are owned and maintained by the Martha's Vineyard Land Bank Commission, an organization funded by a 2 percent fee added to all real estate transactions. One of the motivations for the Land Bank's purchases of Ripley's Field and Tisbury Meadow Preserves was to maintain open meadows and protect the variety of rare plants, birds, and animals that live there. Because open areas on Martha's Vineyard are either farmed or overgrown by trees, meadows have become ecologically rare communities.

The fields in the Tisbury Meadow property had been farmland; the original farmhouse sits next to the parking lot. The long, narrow ridge in the center of the property is an example of an esker, shaped during the period of glacial melting when streams of water poured off the glacier. Sand and gravel that the ice sheet picked up as it inched its way southward streamed off to form this high ridge. The dirt road that cuts through the southern section of the preserve is called the "Old Road to Holmes Hole." In the eighteenth century it served as the main thoroughfare for carts to transport goods and families from one end of the island to the other.

THE ROUTE

Tisbury Meadow Preserve

1. From the parking lot, turn left onto the Orange Trail. Haul your bike up the stairs and remain on the Orange Trail.

    On the left side of the path you'll see the rambling **multiflora rose**, whose small white flowers become shiny red rose hips in the autumn.

2. At the junction with the Blue Trail, turn right. (If you remain on the Orange Trail, you will end up on Old Holmes Hole Road).

3. Take your next left onto the Red Trail.

    This path travels through typical Vineyard forest consisting of tall, stately oak trees towering over huckleberry and blueberry bushes. The best picking is in early August.

4. At the fork bear left, heading onto the Yellow Trail. The path climbs up and down, the result of glacial action that took place thousands of years ago.

5. Cross Old Holmes Hole Road, the cart path where horse-drawn carriages traveled between up-island towns and down-island communities,

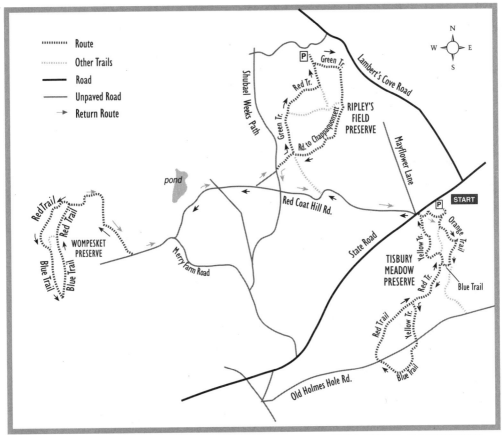

TISBURY MEADOW — WOMPESKET–RIPLEY'S FIELD PRESERVES

and pick up the Blue Trail. The Blue Trail loops around, changing from single- to double-track.

6. Cross another section of the old carriage road onto the Red Trail.

7. At the intersection with the Yellow Trail, remain on the Red, retracing your route.

8. Upon reaching the meadow, turn left onto the Yellow Trail.

> A large **viburnum** bush, which in early summer produces large clusters of white flowers, grows on the left corner. Also on your left is a common island shrub called **sheep laurel** or **lambkill**. This benign name, sheep laurel, is appropriate for the beautiful clusters of pink

flowers that bloom in June. However, farmers call the shrub lambkill because many livestock die after nibbling on its poisonous leaves.

Birdhouses in the meadow draw assorted birds whose calls and songs ring through the air. The mockingbird's song is the most distinctive, with many different phrases linked together. The prairie warbler trills from low to high, and the song sparrow whistles a melodious tune.

Butterfly weed

Wide patches of **velvet grass** color the meadow in tones of pink. The velvet grass intermingles with small purple wildflowers called **dame's violet**. In summer the field is awash with the brilliant orange **butterfly weed**. Its name is derived from its popularity with the monarch butterfly, which feeds on its small blossoms. Native Americans called this plant pleurisy root because they believed that chewing on its tough stem would cure them of pleurisy, a lung disease that plagued early settlers.

9. Continue straight on the Yellow Trail as it meets State Road. (If you wish to return to the parking lot, turn right.)

10. Cross State Road onto the dirt road (Mayflower Lane).

11. Take an immediate left, passing the Land Bank marker and traveling through the stone barricade onto Red Coat Hill Road.

Red Coat Hill Road is another one of the Vineyard's "ancient ways." If you compare the height of the road to the terrain on either side, you'll notice how low the road is—the result of generations of Vineyarders traveling this route.

Hundreds of years ago, when the Vineyard consisted mainly of farmland, the view from the highest point on this road included a clear shot of Vineyard Haven Harbor. This lookout was vital to the island's defense against the threat of British invasion during the Revolutionary War. However, in September 1778, General Sir Charles Grey led his British, redcoated expeditionary force brigadiers up the road, and they seized this high ground. The road's name continues to be a reminder of this historic event.

12. Remain on Red Coat Hill Road for 0.9 mile, crossing all intersections, until you reach a paved road (Merry Farm Road). Turn right.

13. Pedal up Merry Farm Road as it changes from pavement to dirt. Then continue about 500 feet and look on the right for the Land Bank marker and the sign for Wompesket Preserve. Just before the road forks, turn right onto the path that skirts the edge of what used to be the old Merry Farm.

Look to your left at the unusually shaped oak tree standing alone in the meadow. Its misshapen limbs result from continual gusts of salt-laden winds. Beyond the tree is a view of the island's north shore and Vineyard Sound.

Wompesket Preserve

This property, although much smaller than the other two, is more diverse. While biking or hiking through wetlands and woods, along ponds and into a meadow, you'll experience a variety of ecosystems. Be prepared to dismount at stream crossings.

14. Head down the hill to the wetlands.

On the right grows a large plant with a wide red stalk supporting great clusters of small purple berries. **Pokeweed** is an extremely poisonous plant. Its berries produce a bright purple juice used in inks and dyes.

The trail crosses into a wet wooded area with the tangled, thorny **greenbrier** growing all around. **Sweet pepperbush,** whose fragrant, white spiky flowers perfume the air, is also typical wetland vegetation.

Just before the stone wall look for **swamp azaleas** displaying their lovely white trumpet-shaped flowers.

15. Bear right at the fork onto the Red Trail.

This trail winds through a forest of large oak trees. The age of the oaks, about 60 to 70 years, indicates the period of elapsed time since this land was used for farming.

At the top of an arid knoll sits a split-rail bench, a convenient rest stop at the halfway point of this exploration. Here the ground is covered with pale green **lichen**, a prehistoric vegetation that can survive in dry, windblown areas. The fuzzy green ground cover growing nearby is named **haircap moss** and grows in more-sheltered spots.

After you cross another bridge, look to the left at a **chokecherry** tree that is split down the middle. Although the center of the tree has died, one half continues to grow to the right, while the other half sprouts out to the left.

16. At the intersection with the Blue Trail, bear right onto it.

   Pedal (or attempt to—the grass here is often quite high) through the meadow until you reach a small pond and the end of the trail. If you're lucky enough to be biking in August when blackberries are in season, stay and snack from the bushes that grow on both sides of the trail.

17. Reverse direction and fork right to return to the opposite side of the meadow.

   Many **Russian olive** trees grow here. An introduced species, this shrub, with its long slender leaves and silvery undersurfaces, has proliferated on the island.

   In the meadow you'll observe an unusual growth pattern: several chokecherry trees with multiple stems. Look for the tree that has sixteen separate stems growing from one stump. A possible explanation for this phenomenon is that the field was mowed many times during the trees' early growing period, and each time the trees' tops were chopped off, they sprouted other stems.

18. On the return leg of the hike, keep to the right, traveling first on the Blue Trail and then on the Red.

19. From the preserve, retrace your route back down the Merry Farm Road.

20. Turn left onto Red Coat Hill Road.

21. Remain on Red Coat Hill Road for 0.3 mile. Turn left at the second major intersection (just after Cranberry Acres) onto Shubael Weeks Path. A reference point to verify you are at the correct intersection is an electric transformer box, No. 86010, sitting in front of a house on the right side of the road.

22. After 0.1 mile you may see a sign for Ripley's Field Preserve. Take the next right onto the Road to Chappaquonsett.

23. Follow the road to a three-pronged fork. Turn left onto the Green Trail.

Ripley's Field Preserve

The topography of Ripley's Field is similar to Tisbury Meadow: open meadow leading to hilly woodland. You are approaching Ripley's Field through the "back door." Your ride heads first into woodland, then into meadow and back to woodland. This preserve is great for biking, but watch out for tree roots and stumps that often pop up on the trail.

24. Remain on the Green Trail that suddenly changes to the Red Trail.

> The trail borders a field filled with wildflowers and pink-hued velvet grass.

25. At the junction with another Red Trail, bear left as the path skirts a horse farm.

> The path leaves a forest of oak trees and meanders into a meadow filled with wildflowers such as the tiny, purple-blossomed **vetch**; **hawkweed**, with its small yellow flowers; and **bird's-foot trefoil**, which is also yellow but produces larger blooms.

26. After passing through the meadow, turn left onto the Red Trail, re-entering a woodland filled with tall pines and oak trees.

27. Don't miss the next intersection (I always do), where you turn right onto the Green Trail (a left turn leads to the parking lot). Remain on the Green Trail as the path ascends steeply through the forest, descends, and then crosses a dirt road.

28. Turn right at the next dirt road, the Road to Chappaquonsett.

29. Remain on the road until you return to the intersection with Shubael Weeks Path. Turn left.

30. Turn left at the intersection onto Red Coat Hill Road.

31. Remain on Red Coat Hill Road until it ends at Mayflower Lane. Turn right to cross State Road.

32. Re-enter Tisbury Meadow Preserve and turn left onto the Yellow Trail to return to the parking lot.

CHAPTER FOURTEEN

Waskosim's Rock Reservation

At 185 acres, Waskosim's Rock Reservation boasts the largest acreage of any Martha's Vineyard Land Bank property. Its well-maintained trails through varied terrain filled with a mix of wildflowers, birds, and trees make it a favorite of bikers and hikers.

The reservation is named after an immense boulder that dominates one of the highest hills on the Vineyard. A huge crack running down the middle of Waskosim's Rock has inspired numerous local legends and created many photo opportunities.

Directions: The reservation is located off the left side of North Road, 1.5 miles west of the junction with State Road and just after the Chilmark town line sign.

Distance: 4.5 miles.

Difficulty: Moderate.

Food and drink: The Vineyard Food Shop is 1.5 miles west, at the intersection of State, North, and South Roads in West Tisbury.

Background: Waskosim's Rock and all the smaller boulders that surround it were deposited by a receding glacier. The rock's original silhouette was altered by a bolt of lightning, which created a fissure large enough to conceal two or three people. Rumor has it that Waskosim's Rock was once a favorite hideaway for fugitives.

The Indian Chiefs Nashawakemmuck and Takemmy probably gave the rock its name when they began the tradition of having the boulder serve as a boundary between their properties. Matthew Mayhew, a Vineyard settler, continued this tradition by using the rock to separate his land from that of the Wampanoag. This boundary, called the Middle Line, was defined by a stone wall that ran straight, from the rock to Menemsha Pond. The land to the north of the line belonged to the Wampanoag, and to the south, Mayhew.

THE ROUTE

1. From the parking lot, head onto the Blue Trail.

2. At the intersection posted with No. 32, turn left, remaining on the Blue Trail. You may have to walk your bike over the boardwalk of hand-hewn cedar planks.

> This wetland contains many species of moisture-loving plants. The **sweet pepperbush,** with its spiky white flowers which perfume the summer air, and the **swamp azalea**, whose white blooms give off a cinnamon-like odor, are two of the more pleasant smelling plants. One that doesn't smell as pleasant is found growing low to the ground next to the boardwalk. If you sniff the underside of the **skunk cabbage's** large leaves where they connect to its fleshy stem, you'll know how it got its name. **Cinnamon ferns**, which thrive in damp areas, line the sides of the trail. At the end of the bridge, a grove of **wild sarsaparilla** line the trail. Look for an umbrella-shaped leaf with three layers. In the summer, clusters of greenish white flowers hide below the leaves.

Wooden steps that protect old stone walls require that you haul your bike up and over. Your reward is a technically challenging stretch over tree roots, rocks, and hunks of granite. On your left, the Mill Brook parallels the path.

This trail meanders back and forth over the brook amid groves
of maple and beech trees. **American holly** trees and **sassafras** trees
with mitten-shaped leaves also grow alongside the trail.

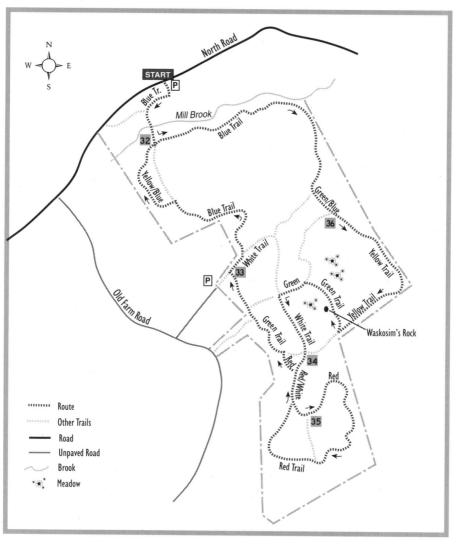

⚙️ WASKOSIM'S ROCK RESERVATION

3. Turn left onto the Green/Blue Trail.

The trail runs by a stone wall and cuts through a meadow criss-crossed by many stone walls. The walls are remnants from the days when stones lying in the fields were piled on top of each other to contain cows and sheep that grazed the land. The foundation sitting in the meadow belonged to the Allen family, who farmed the land more than one hundred years ago.

Bird feeders scattered across the meadow draw a variety of birds, including doves, bobwhites, starlings, robins, swallows, goldfinches, crows, and hawks in search of prey.

In late summer or autumn, you may see fuzzy white clusters of small flowers named **hyssop-leaved thoroughwort**, also known as **boneset.** The name boneset came from herb doctors, who used the plant to heal broken bones. **Queen Anne's lace** blooms all summer, displaying flat-topped clusters of tiny, white flowers. Its leaves resemble those of its ancestor, the carrot. Like the carrot, its long taproot can be cooked and eaten. **Sweeteverlasting** displays clusters of small flowers, white with yellow centers in late summer and early fall. Its name probably comes from the fragrant scent that the plant gives off when crushed. (Please do not test this hypothesis, or sweetever-

Sweeteverlasting &
Bladder campion

lasting will not "live" up to its name). **Bladder campion**, with white flowers atop a bladderlike cup, also grows here. The center of the meadow is filled with white **daisies**, which are surrounded by the pink-hued velvet grass.

4. At the next fork (which may be marked by a No. 36), continue straight onto the Yellow Trail. Be alert to yellow Land Bank route markers attached to trees. The path leaves the meadow and heads into the woods.

    The small, lacy, delicate fern growing in the shady areas is called **maidenhair fern**.

    In summer, juicy black huckleberries growing on both sides of the trail provide an energy boost for tackling the upcoming hills. As you head up the first incline, make sure you keep your balance and don't fall into the large patch of poison ivy growing beside the path.

5. After the second short incline, bear right at the fork onto the Green Trail. **Waskosim's Rock** is about 500 feet ahead on the right.

    A 6-foot-square, flat-topped boulder near the base of the rock makes a perfect picnic table. Farther up the trail on your right may be a view (in early spring and late fall when there is no foliage on the trees) of the Vineyard Sound foothills, including the adjacent Mill Brook and surrounding valley. This deep, narrow valley was known for generations as Zephaniah's Holler, named after Captain Zephaniah Mayhew, one of the early settlers on Martha's Vineyard.

    Many years ago, when the Vineyard consisted mainly of farmland and was not so densely forested, Waskosim's Rock could be seen from a great distance and was a popular visiting place. Farmers brought their families to the site to picnic and enjoy the view.

6. Continue past the rock and bear left, remaining on the Green Trail.

7. Turn left at the fork, still on the Green Trail.

8. Take your next left, heading back into the meadow, now on the White Trail.

    This old carriage road ascends, passing numerous large granite boulders. A glimpse to the northeast one hundred years ago would have revealed distant ocean views. Now the only view consists of water towers amid the foliage.

Waskosim's Rock, the mighty boulder that has inspired more
than a few legends—and photo opportunities.

9. At the fork bear right to remain on the White Trail through the No. 34 intersection.

10. Continue straight on the White Trail until the intersection with the Red/White Trail. Bear left.

11. Turn left at No. 35 onto the Red Trail. This is a great cycling loop. The single-track climbs and then descends amidst an understory of ferns, huckleberries, and poison ivy. Toward the end of the loop, watch for poison ivy near the remnants of a stone wall.

12. After completing the loop and reriding the Red/White Trail, turn left onto the Red Trail, where you again must haul your bike over another protected stone wall.

13. Take the next left onto the Green Trail.

14. Bear right at the fork, remaining on the Green Trail as it continues to ascend.

15. Bear left, staying on the Green Trail as it crosses a small plank bridge. The path leaves the woods and enters a sandy, gravelly section, passing by the west side of the meadow you pedaled through earlier in the ride.

16. Turn right onto the White Trail. A left turn leads to another entrance to the reservation from Old Farm Road.

17. Take the next left onto the Blue Trail. (No. 33 is attached to a tree on the right side of the intersection.)

18. Turn left onto the Yellow/Blue Trail, a narrow, single-track path.

A large handsome **beech** tree with its smooth, light-gray bark stands next to the path at the end of your descent. The vine winding itself around the tree is called **Virginia creeper**. It attaches itself by means of tiny tendrils, each with an adhesive disc at its end. In autumn it produces poisonous berries that cluster at the end of its branches.

19. Turn left at No. 32 to return to the parking lot.

CHAPTER FIFTEEN

Edgartown—Lighthouse Beach

Edgartown possesses a rare combination of charm, history, and beauty. To fully appreciate Edgartown's assets, stroll down its narrow streets lined with majestic, old, meticulously landscaped homes. After inspecting the center, head for the coast and Lighthouse Beach. While walking along the beach to Eel Pond, you may notice other aspects of the town: elegant captains' homes perched above the shore, boats sailing in and out of Edgartown Harbor, and the rustic coasts of Chappaquiddick and Cape Poge.

Wear your bathing suit. Swimming, shelling, sunbathing, and picnicking are at hand on this unspoiled stretch of sand.

Directions: If you are arriving by car, forget hunting for a parking place (with a one-hour time limit) and park in the free outlying lots. The Triangle lot is located off the Edgartown–Vineyard Haven Road, just west of the triangle intersection with Beach Road. A second lot is across from the elementary school on Robinson Road, situated between the Edgartown–West Tisbury Road and Pease's Point Way. If you park in the Robinson Road lot, you can walk 0.3 mile to the starting point of the tour or take the trolley that runs every fifteen minutes. The Triangle lot (also with trolley) is 0.5 mile from the starting point.

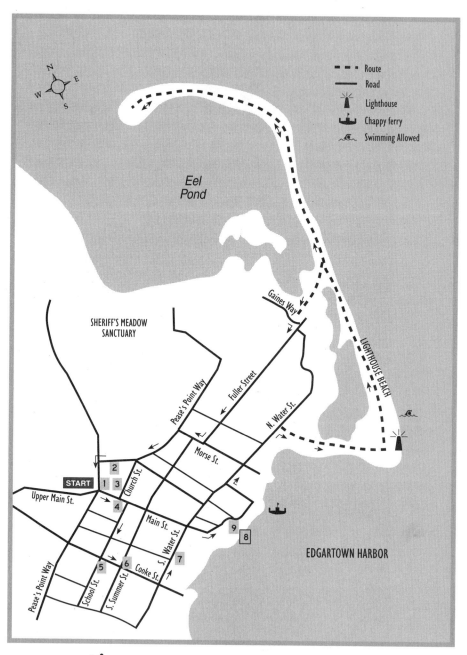

Route

Road

Lighthouse

Chappy ferry

Swimming Allowed

Eel Pond

SHERIFF'S MEADOW SANCTUARY

Gaines Way

Pease's Point Way

Fuller Street

N. Water St.

LIGHTHOUSE BEACH

Morse St.

START

Upper Main St.

Church St.

Main St.

S. Water St.

Pease's Point Way

School St.

S. Summer St.

Cooke St.

EDGARTOWN HARBOR

🚶🚶 EDGARTOWN – LIGHTHOUSE BEACH

Distance: 3.4 miles to explore the town and beach; 1.7 miles to tour the town.

Difficulty: Easy, level walking.

Restrooms: On the left side of the visitor center on Church Street, which runs between Main Street and Pease's Point Way.

Food and drink: Among the Flowers Cafe on Mayhew Lane, off North Water Street (reasonably priced outdoor dining); Mad Martha's, North Water Street (ice cream, grinders).

Fees: Vincent House, the Vineyard Museum.

Background: Edgartown owes its prosperous beginnings to the whaling industry. Many of the English settlers who sailed to Martha's Vineyard in 1642 were familiar with whaling; others learned from the Wampanoag tribe, who had been whaling for centuries. The Wampanoag killed whales for their meat, but the English were mainly after blubber, which contained a valuable oil used for illumination and lubrication.

Edgartown was one of New England's primary nineteenth-century whaling ports. Its handsome homes were constructed during this period by residents who prospered due to the whaling industry. By 1860, however, petroleum and its derivatives had begun to replace whale oil, the main product delivered by whaling ships to ports up and down the coast. This reduced demand for whale byproducts, coupled with a diminishing whale population, forced Edgartown residents to turn from whaling to the less remunerative occupations of fishing and navigating. Fortunately, Edgartown has carefully preserved the character of this nineteenth-century whaling era.

THE ROUTE

1. Begin at the intersection of Pease's Point Way and Main Street, and head east on Main Street.

    Look on your left for the **Daniel Fisher House** (1 on the map). The simple yet elegant style of this home, with its symmetry and delicately carved mantels and moldings, is characteristic of the fine craftsmanship exhibited during the Federal period. Although Harvard-educated Daniel Fisher arrived on the island in 1824 intending to practice medicine, he eventually became the Vineyard's most successful businessman. He was a whale oil merchant who owned and operated the largest spermaceti (whale oil extract) candle factory in the world. As founder and first president of the Martha's Vineyard National Bank, Dr. Fisher became part owner of many whaling vessels. He also ran a whale oil refinery, a hardtack bakery that supplied whalers, and a grist-mill in West Tisbury, and he even managed to squeeze in a medical practice. He was described in 1857 as "the tallest, stongest-built, healthiest, and handsomest, as well as the wealthiest and most influential, inhabitant of Martha's Vineyard." The house built for him is now owned by the Martha's Vineyard Preservation Trust and is a popular spot for weddings.

The historic Daniel Fisher House.

2.   Walk behind the Daniel Fisher House to visit the simple, functional **Vincent House** (2), one of the oldest unaltered homes on the Vineyard.

Built by William Vincent in 1672 near the shore of Edgartown Great Pond, it housed generations of Vincents until it was sold in 1941. The house was moved in 1977 and then carefully restored. The restorers deliberately left part of the interior unfinished so visitors can view the method of construction used in these early homes. Each of three rooms is furnished to represent a century of island life. Run by the Martha's Vineyard Preservation Trust, the Vincent House is open daily, except Sunday, from May 1 through October 15.

3. From the Vincent house, cut through the parking lot in back of the **Old Whaling Church** (3) and turn right on Church Street.

Old whaling church.

The Old Whaling Church is a fine example of Greek Revival architecture, with its distinctive imposing columns interspersed with four large Gothic windows. This handsome structure, one of three churches designed by Frederick Baylies Jr. of Edgartown, was constructed in the same manner as a whaling ship. Fifty-foot red pine beams support the structure, which in 1843 was the largest on the island. The light in its 92-foot tower could be seen far across the sea and served as a beacon for returning sailors. However, its large Methodist congregation gradually dwindled, and the church became the property of the Martha's Vineyard Preservation Trust. Elegant old whale oil lamps, now electrified, illuminate the 500-seat building, which now functions as both a church and a performing arts center.

4. From Main Street take your first right onto School Street. To the right, at No. 20, sits the second church designed by Baylies in 1839 (4). Formerly a **Baptist church**, it is now a private residence.

5. Walk two blocks and turn left on Cooke Street.

At the corner of School and Cooke Streets stand four buildings owned and operated by the Martha's Vineyard Historical Society. **The Vineyard Museum** (5), which includes the Cooke House and Foster Maritime Gallery, is open during the summer, Tuesday through Saturday, from 10:00 A.M. to 5:00 P.M. There is an entrance fee.

Thomas Cooke, a businessman and the Edgartown customs collector, built the House in 1765 to house his office and family. Much of the eleven-room residence, including many of the windowpanes, has remained unchanged. Inside, exhibits feature collections of historic relics, including Native American artifacts, costumes, household goods, and marble headstones from the graves of two favorite chickens that belonged to Nancy Luce, an eccentric former resident of West Tisbury.

The Gale Huntington Library of History and the Foster Gallery are located in the main building. Inside the library hangs a portrait of wealthy Dr. Daniel Fisher. More than 10,000 books on Vineyard history and more than 100 logbooks from whaling vessels line the walls. The gallery displays items from the island's marine history such as scrimshaw from whaling trips, ship models, and paintings.

A third building houses a hand-pumped 1852 fire engine, a peddler's cart, a racing boat, and a Nomans Land boat, while the Francis Pease House contains the children's museum, museum shop, and restrooms. The brick tower in the middle of the lawn holds the gigantic Fresnel lens from the old Gay Head Lighthouse.

6. Turn right on Cooke Street toward the waterfront. On the left side, where Summer Street intersects Cooke, stands the Baylies-designed **Federated Church** (6), built in 1828. Baptist-Congregational services are held each Sunday in its spartan sanctuary, the oldest on the island. Look in the windows to see hanging whale oil lamps, an old organ, and enclosed pews designed to trap heat during cold winter months.

7. Continue on Cooke Street for another block until you reach South Water Street. Turn left and walk one and a half blocks to the Captain Thomas Milton House on the right. Now owned by the Harborside Inn, the residence was built by Milton, a retired sea captain who made most of his money by investing in Edgartown real estate. In 1840 he built this house next to the Flame Tree, planted in 1834, which he had purchased as a seedling on one of his whaling trips to China. This huge, handsome tree is known as the **pagoda tree** (7) and is said to be the oldest one on this continent.

    Proceed up South Water Street to the heart of the business district. Locals complain about the number of shops selling T-shirts, but there also are many stores carrying unusual handcrafted items.

8. Take the first right back onto Main Street to proceed to the waterfront.

9. Turn left to reach **Memorial Wharf** (8), the town dock once owned by Dr. Fisher.

    Located on the water beyond a cluster of stores the wharf features and observation deck you can climb to view a magnificent seascape encompassing Cape Poge to the left, Chappaquiddick ahead, Katama Bay to the right, and Edgartown Harbor in the foreground.

    Across the street from the wharf sits a small park dedicated to whales. Among the items displayed is a life-size sculpture of a whale's tail rendered by Ovid Osborton Ward in honor of his great-grandfather, who owned whaling ships. Next to the park sits the **Old Sculpin Gallery** (9). This quaint building originally belonged to entrepreneurial Dr. Fisher and was part of his whale oil refinery. After the demise of the whale oil industry, the building became a boat shop. This edifice has changed little during the last 200 years. If you step inside you can see the old floor and weathered beams, along with pictures painted by Vineyard artists.

Just past Memorial Wharf, on the right, is the ferry to Chappaquiddick. During the busy summer months two ferries, each transporting bicycles, foot passengers, and three vehicles, continually shuttle back and forth across the narrow channel. Since one or the other ferry is always at or near one of the two docks, they are aptly named "On Time."

10. From the ferry dock, turn left and travel up Daggett Street past the line of cars waiting for their turn to travel across the water to Chappaquiddick.

11. Turn right onto North Water Street to view the stately old Federal-style homes positioned at an angle to the street so that their occupants would have a better view of boats sailing into the harbor. On the roofs are widow's walks, or parapets, surrounded by balustrade railings, from which watchful spouses awaited the return of their seafaring husbands.

Many of these homes were built between 1830 and 1850, when the whaling industry was at its peak. Their uniformity of color, proper sense of proportion, and elegant architectural details combine to create one of the most aesthetically pleasing avenues on the Vineyard. No. 86, which belonged to Captain Jared Fisher, is one of the most elegant homes. Its Greek-Revival style indicates that it was built at the same time as the Daniel Fisher House.

Peek into the side and back yards of these homes to see carefully cultivated gardens, where a variety of colorful blooms thrive in the moist salt air.

The imposing building situated on the corner of North Water Street and Starbuck Neck Road is the Harbor View Hotel, built in the 1890s. The first large hotel built on the island, it was instrumental in the conversion of Edgartown to a resort community. Across the street from the hotel is a path leading to the lighthouse.

12. Turn right onto the path to the **Edgartown Lighthouse**, located at the entrance to Edgartown Harbor.

Originally the lighthouse was built in 1828 on a man-made island of granite blocks connected by a wooden walkway to the mainland. The walkway was replaced by a causeway which became unnecessary when

The Edgartown Lighthouse and its namesake beach in the foreground.

strong water currents created a small barrier beach and sandy access strip.

The seascape to your right reveals windsurfers' brightly colored sails weaving around anchored yachts, sailboats racing across the bay, and the On Time ferries shuttling back and forth to Chappaquiddick. The view toward Chappaquiddick includes bathers at the Chappy Beach Club, fishermen, and wood-shingled homes straddling the bluffs.

The multifaceted landscape up toward the captains' homes begins with yachts attached to docks and small boathouses hugging the water.

13.   Head left down the mile-long stretch toward Eel Pond, where you'll have a closer view of narrow Cape Poge.

This isolated peninsula is accessible only by boat or by driving 7 miles on a sandy beach. The abundance of fish in Cape Poge Bay draws not only fishermen but also flocks of sea gulls that breed on its uninhabited western tip. If you make the trip to Cape Poge in June, beware of divebombing mother gulls protecting their young.

Eel Pond is great for kayaking (chapter 34) and a favorite island spot for shellfishing. Among the varieties of shells found on the beach are

Quahog, mussel, scallop

hard, round **quahog** shells; small, fragile **steamer** shells; black, oval **mussel** shells; and ridged, fan-shaped **scallop** shells. Low tide draws clammers raking and plunging for these succulent mollusks. Each town has its own shellfish warden, who issues permits for clamming and scalloping and also polices the local waters.

The beach bends toward Eel Pond. At the tip of the beach you can view Oak Bluffs to the north. The Cape Poge Lighthouse sits off to the east on an elbow of land.

14. Retrace your steps back down the beach toward the harbor.

15. After walking about 0.5 mile, look on the right for the path that links the beach with the town. Walk up that path to Gaines Way.

16. Turn left onto Gaines Way.

17. Turn right onto Fuller Street. Flower lovers should watch for colorful gardens hiding behind fences.

18. Fuller ends at Morse Street. Turn right.

19. At the next block Morse intersects with Pease's Point Way. Turn left.

20. Follow Pease's Point Way past the bike racks and trolley stop, as it bends left and then intersects with Upper Main Street.

21. Turn right on Upper Main Street to return to the starting point.

CHAPTER SIXTEEN

Sheriff's Meadow Sanctuary

Sheriff's Meadow is located right in the center of Edgartown, but this small scenic sanctuary hosts a range of natural communities usually found in remote areas. Here you'll find meadow and woodland, freshwater pond and saltwater marsh—diverse environments supporting a wide variety of flora and fauna. The sanctuary's trails wind through lush foliage, revealing views across Eel Pond to Nantucket Sound and Chappaquiddick. Perhaps, because of the contrast between serene Sheriff's Meadow and the hustle and bustle of Edgartown, the variety and number of birdcalls is all the more noticeable. Bring your binoculars on your walk so that you can spot birds such as black-bellied plovers, red-winged blackbirds, or great blue herons. You also may glimpse a raccoon crawling through the brush or several swans flying from one body of water to the next.

Directions: To reach the sanctuary from the Main Street side of Cannonball (Memorial) Park in Edgartown, go north on Pease's Point Way. Continue straight on Pease's Point Way, which then becomes Planting Field Way. Proceed 0.2 mile down Planting Field Way. Look for the small Sheriff's Meadow sign on the right side of the road.

Distance: 0.5 mile.

Difficulty: Easy.

Food and drink: On Upper Main Street near Cannonball Park: Soigné on the south side of the road for takeout, or Village Rotisserie on the north side. Edgartown Center offers many choices.

Restrooms: Located on the left side of the visitor center on Church Street, which lies between Main Street and Pease's Point Way.

Background: In 1958 Henry Beetle Hough, an influential and respected island resident who for many years was editor and publisher of the weekly *Vineyard Gazette*, purchased ten acres of land surrounding Sheriff's Pond. In order to protect this property from future development, Henry and his wife, Betty, created the Sheriff's Meadow Foundation. During the next fifteen years other landowners donated six additional acres to the sanctuary. Today the Sheriff's Meadow Foundation has grown into a conservation organization with island holdings covering more than 2,000 acres.

The function of the Sheriff's Meadow Foundation is to "preserve, administer, and maintain natural habitats for wild life on Martha's Vineyard for educational purposes and in the interests of conservation." In order to protect its properties from overuse, it does not allow swimming, picnicking, or biking on them. The foundation's hope is that visitors enter these properties to quietly commune with nature.

THE ROUTE

1. Proceed down this narrow, overgrown path lined with **eastern white pine** and spruce trees.

2. The trail forks just as you enter a meadow. Go left.

    You will pass several large **white oak** trees with smooth, pale gray trunks. Baby **Norway spruce** trees grow under the canopy of pine and **northern white cedar** trees.

    Watch for poison ivy along the path as it bends, crossing between John Butler's Mudhole on the left and Sheriff's Pond on the right. Sheriff's Pond and the sanctuary were named for Isaiah Pease, a former owner of this property, who was sheriff of Duke's County from 1822 until his death in 1862. The sheriff sold ice from this freshwater pond for refrigeration and built an icehouse nearby where he cut and stored the ice.

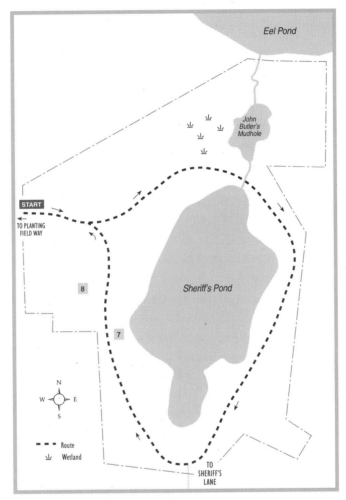

🚶🚶 SHERIFF'S MEADOW SANCTUARY

Beyond the Mudhole lies Eel Pond (great for kayaking; see chapter 34), which is encircled by Little Beach. If you look far out onto Nantucket Sound you'll spot the Cape Poge Lighthouse on an elbow of land connected to Chappaquiddick by a stretch of barrier beach.

Peeking out from the marsh grass is **sea lavender**. Its name refers to the color of its tiny flowers which bloom in late summer and early fall. Also flowering in autumn is **seaside goldenrod**. Its small bright-yellow flowers form a long cluster at the top. The **groundsel tree** favors these marshy areas. In late summer and early fall it produces clusters of small white, feathery flowers.

Shadbush

As you proceed around the west side of the pond, you'll notice that the vegetation becomes very dense. A grove of **shadbush** forms a canopy over the path. **Pasture rose** and **multifora rose** reach out, hooking the unsuspecting walker with their thorny branches. Other non-native plant species, with their junglelike density of vines, stems, and runners, are crowding out native species. The Sheriff's Meadow Foundation is attempting to reduce an invasion of Asiatic bittersweet, Japanese honeysuckle, and porcelain berry.

Remain on the main trail while passing side paths to private homes and to the tennis courts at the Edgartown Yacht Club.

Look on the right for a **tamarack** tree, a conifer that sheds its leaves in the winter. This tree is easy to spot because its slender needles grow in large tufts that shoot out at the ends of stunted branches. Native Americans used the tough fibers from its roots to bind the seams of their birch-bark canoes. The wood of the tamarack tree is now used for poles and lumber. You will not find many other tamarack trees on Martha's Vineyard, as this species prefers a colder climate.

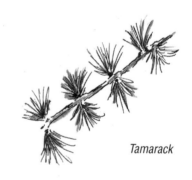

Tamarack

On the right, a cleared area encourages a stop at the edge of the pond to view the wildlife, such as snapping and painted turtles and muskrats. Swans, mallards, and Canada geese often paddle around searching for food, while kingfishers and cormorants swoop down to hunt their prey.

John Butler's Mudhole and Eel Pond.

3. Pass the left fork, which leads to private residences, and follow the trail through a pine forest.

4. At the next fork turn right toward the pond. A bench perched near the water's edge provides a resting place to appreciate this tranquil setting.

A boardwalk lies between a No. 7 marker on the right and a No. 8 on the left. No. 7 refers to **swamp loosestrife,** a tall plant that produces small fuschia flowers in the summer. No. 8 marks a **shrub swamp** where the water level rises during very wet spells. Species that grow here, such as highbush blueberry, swamp azalea, and sweet pepperbush, thrive in these semimoist conditions.

5. Return to the main trail to continue the loop.

Sensitive fern, which also prefers a moist environment, grows beside the trail.

6. Bear left to return to the entrance of the sanctuary.

CHAPTER SEVENTEEN

Caroline Tuthill Wildlife Preserve

The Caroline Tuthill Wildlife Preserve is just a stone's throw from the hustle and bustle of the Triangle shopping area, but its hiking trails through 150 acres of pine forest and meadow give it the feeling of being far removed from civilization. This preserve, administered by the low-profile Sheriff's Meadow Foundation, is one of Martha's Vineyard's hidden treasures. Even longtime residents are not aware of its hiking trails along the shore of scenic Sengekontacket Pond and the opportunities for bird-watching around the salt marsh. If you are looking for a conveniently located spot with varied but untaxing terrain that offers fields of lady's slippers in the spring and succulent blueberries in the summer, head for the Tuthill Preserve.

Directions: From the Triangle intersection at Beach Road, travel west 0.4 mile on the Edgartown–Vineyard Haven Road, or travel 3.7 miles east from the "blinker" at Barnes Road. The preserve and its small parking area are located on the north side of the road.

Distance: 1.3 miles.

Difficulty: Easy, mostly level walking with a few short inclines.

Food and drink: The Triangle shopping area has several fast-food restaurants.

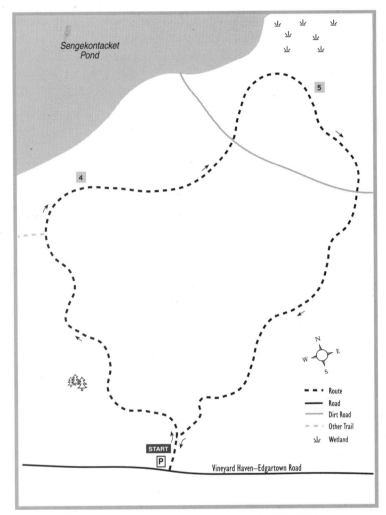

🚶🚶 CAROLINE TUTHILL WILDLIFE PRESERVE

Background: John and Nora Tuthill donated 154 acres of land in memory of their daughter, Caroline, to the Sheriff's Meadow Foundation, a conservation agency that preserves, administers, and maintains natural habitats for wildlife.

As you walk through the preserve, you'll notice several chasms. These deep depressions are called kettle holes and were formed by glacial action. About 15,000 years ago, when the glacier that covered the northeastern section of the

United States started to recede, immense blocks of ice broke off. These blocks then became buried in all the debris that the glacier had picked up on its southward journey. Because these huge chunks melted more slowly than the rest of the ice, they left large depressions in the earth. Some of these kettle holes were so deep that they filled with water and became small inland ponds.

THE ROUTE

1. Begin on the path behind the signpost.

 Soon after you begin your hike you'll notice pine sprouts on both sides of the trail. These sprouts reveal why **pitch pine** trees grow all over the island. Underneath the sprouts are pine tree stumps, and just below the stumps are large root systems. Because these large, vigorous roots grow close to the surface, they can quickly issue new sprouts in an open area where fire or wind has destroyed older pines.

2. Bear left on the trail that winds through a grove of oaks and then pines.

 If you are walking in late May or early June, glance under the pine trees for **lady's slippers**, orchids that grow only in acidic soil. Pine needles from the large number of pine tress contribute to the acidity so thousands of lady's slippers bloom in this preserve, but their delicate pink blossoms are scarce elsewhere. They are practically impossible to propagate and almost equally difficult to pollinate. Lady's slippers do not reward pollinators with nectar. The plant must rely on a not-so-smart bumblebee to enter through a small slit in its slipperlike pouch and then proceed deep within the flower to find the anther. When the nectarless bee exits through a hole in the rear wall of the flower, it rubs against the anther, which then releases the pollen. If the bee is to deposit the pollen, it must go on the same unrewarding search in another lady's slipper. During the summer you will see only pollinated plants because they keep their shriveled seedpods. Unpollinated plants plants dry up and die.

 As you walk, watch for crunchy, gray-blue mosslike clumps that grow in open sunny spots. These primitive plants, which have no roots, stems, leaves, or flowers, are a species of lichen called *Cladonia*. They are often found in areas with severe climatic conditions. **Lichens**, which have been around for millions of years, are composed of two separate organisms: fungus and alga. Both organisms work together like a well-coached team, performing different functions that allow survival in hot, arid regions as well as frigid, windblown mountaintops. The fungus supplies moisture and protects the plant, while the alga provides food.

Cladonia feels sharp and brittle if it grows in hot dry conditions or soft and spongy if it has absorbed water. If you have any extra water with you, put a piece of the dry lichen in a cup with a little water. Watch it quickly absorb all the liquid. This nifty moisture-conservation trick demonstrates how lichens can survive during years of drought and extreme heat or cold. *Cladonia* may not mind extreme weather conditions, but it is very fussy about air quality; it refuses to grow in polluted areas. Naturally, Vineyarders are particularly partial to this plant because it reinforces their belief that their unpolluted island provides better living conditions than on the mainland.

Ignore the path emerging on the left and continue walking straight, following the yellow-topped trail markers. During the summer the forest floor is bedecked with **spotted pipsissewa**, a small, ground-hugging wildflower with five white petals and variegated leaves.

The trail approaches Sengekontacket Pond and then bends to the right following the shore. Here you'll have a view of the pond, the beach, Nantucket Sound, and Beach Road. To the north you can see the town of Oak Bluffs perched on the headland that juts out into the water.

As the trail gets closer to the water and the land becomes moister, the vegetation changes (No. 4 marker). The fragrant **sweet pepperbush** exhibits spiky clusters of small, white flowers that perfume the summer air. You may also see **teaberry**, a small evergreen with shiny, waxy, dark-green leaves that is often decorated with bright red berries.

3. Cross a dirt road and continue on the trail until you reach the salt marsh (behind the No. 5 marker).

Plants and algae growing in the marsh provide nutrients for both shellfish and finfish, which in turn draw shorebirds. You may spot **snowy egrets**, which are white with long black legs and bills, or **great blue herons**, with long, curved necks and dagger-like bills.

Mallards also frequent salt marshes. Instead of diving into the water to feed, they tip their heads down, forcing their tails to bob up in the air. The male is easy to spot because he sports a white necklace below his dark-green neck and head.

Mallard

The view from the salt marsh lookout includes two small bodies of water, both named Trapp's Pond. Beyond the ponds, lying far out in Nantucket Sound, is Cape Poge Elbow. This skinny strip of land, extending out from Chappaquidick, is a prime fishing spot and a sea gull spawning area.

After you leave the marsh overlooks, look on the right for four dead oak trees. In the same area you'll see a group of pitch pine saplings that have taken advantage of the newly available sunlight.

4. Cross back over the road and remain on the trail as it passes huckle-berry, blueberry, and bayberry bushes.

During the summer, the **huckleberry**'s small pale flower becomes a dark round berry containing a tiny seed that crunches when chewed. The **blueberry** has a frosty covering and does not crunch. The **bayberry** bush has larger oval leaves, and only the female develops clusters of small, round, hard white berries that are attached directly to the stem. Huckleberries and blueberries provide a tasty snack for the hungry hiker. Bayberries, which remain on the bush all winter, help sustain the island bird population during cold weather.

Just before the trail starts to descend, look for a small **kettle hole** on the left side surrounded by a thicket of highbush blueberries.

5. After climbing up and down a small hill, bear left at the fork to return to the entrance.

CHAPTER EIGHTEEN

Felix Neck Wildlife Sanctuary

Take a walk on the wild side. All manner of wildlife nest, breed, and forage in and around this 350-acre sanctuary. Wild turkey, Canada geese, osprey, or a horseshoe crab may accompany you on wide, level trails along beach and salt marsh, through open fields and woodlands. Birders describe this Massachusetts Audubon Society property as one of the prime island locales for observing more than 100 species of native birds. Felix Neck also provides an assortment of activities, from bird and wildlife identification walks to snorkeling and canoe trips.

Apply plenty of mosquito repellent.

Directions: From the triangle intersection in Edgartown, travel 2 miles west on the Edgartown–Vineyard Haven Road. From its junction with State Road in Vineyard Haven, the distance is 4.2 miles east on the same road. An incised rectangular stone next to a Massachusetts Audubon sign marks the entrance on the north side of the road. Proceed 0.7 mile down the dirt road to the parking lot.

Distance: 2 miles.

Difficulty: Easy, wide, flat trails.

Restrooms: In the vistor center, where you pay your admission fee.

Fees: $3 adult; $2 child; free to members of the Massachusetts Audubon Society. Closed on Mondays. The vistor center contains trail maps, an exhibit room, and a shop selling books and nature-oriented items. The exhibit room features displays as well as fresh- and saltwater aquariums filled with native fish, bivalves, amphibians, and reptiles. Check outside under the barn for barn owls.

Background: Before European settlers arrived on the Vineyard, this land was inhabited by Native Americans who farmed crops such as squash, tobacco, and Jerusalem artichokes. They called this section of the island Weenomset, which means "place of the grape." When the English arrived, they named the land after Felix Kuttashamaquat, a Native American who farmed and grazed his sheep here.

In 1664 Edgartown settlers divided Felix Neck into 25 sections. Among those who received parcels of land were John Smith and William Vincent, ancestors of Walter Smith of Edgartown. For the next three hundred years the Smith family farmed this land. The vistor center stands on the foundation of the Smith family's old horse barn. When Walter's grandfather died, he left all the land to him. In 1963 Walter Smith sold 180 acres to George Moffett for $106,000, with the understanding that Moffett would keep only 40 acres for himself and put the rest of the land in trust so that it would remain forever wild.

In 1964 Moffett permitted the Martha's Vineyard Natural History Society to use the property to run a nature-study program, which continues today and is called Fern and Feather. Five years later he donated all his property to the Massachusetts Audubon Society. Other acquisitions and donations added 170 acres to the sanctuary.

Felix Neck employs naturalists who offer a variety of bird-watching, canoeing, star-gazing, and seashell-identifying excursions. The sanctuary also serves as a summer day camp for children ages four to twelve. But its most important function is to provide a natural habitat for its many varied species of wildlife.

An osprey pole stands next to the entrance road. **Osprey,** which resemble eagles, prefer to nest on top of dead trees near water that holds a plentiful supply of fish. Until recently, a lack of suitable trees prevented osprey from building nests on the island. Gus Ben David, the director of Felix Neck, was

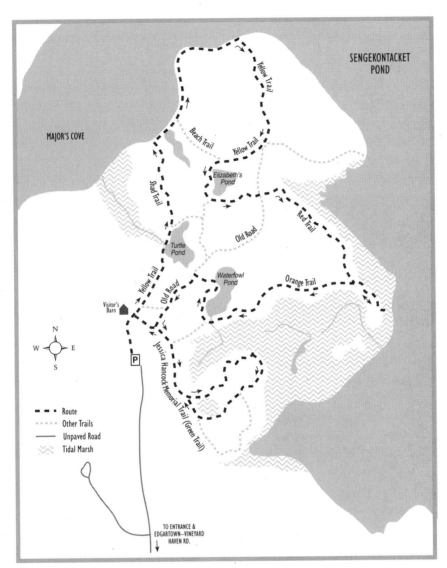

SENGEKONTACKET POND

MAJOR'S COVE

Yellow Trail

Beach Trail

Yellow Trail

Elizabeth's Pond

Shad Trail

Red Trail

Old Road

Turtle Pond

Yellow Trail

Old Road

Waterfowl Pond

Orange Trail

Visitor's Barn

N
W · E
S

P

Jessica Hancock Memorial Trail (Green Trail)

- - - Route
..... Other Trails
——— Unpaved Road
〰〰 Tidal Marsh

TO ENTRANCE &
EDGARTOWN—VINEYARD
HAVEN RD.

🚶🚶 FELIX NECK WILDLIFE SANCTUARY

instrumental in increasing the number of osprey by encouraging the telephone company and local volunteers to erect telephone poles for nesting sites. Poles topped by osprey nests are now located all over the island, including Wasque Reservation, Katama Point, and Long Point. The project was so

successful that now residents must put their names on a waiting list to purchase osprey poles.

THE ROUTE

On your way from the parking lot to the vistor center, stop at the butterfly
garden, where butterflies sip nectar from flowers planted specifically to
attract them. A goldfish pond lies next to the garden. Brightly hued fish swim
among water hyacinths and lilies.

1. Begin your hike on the Yellow Trail, which starts behind the vistor cen-
    ter.

    The field on your right is mowed to provide an environment for
    wildflowers, butterflies, birds, and small mammals. If you are hiking
    during the summer months, watch for the brilliant orange flower called
    butterfly weed. Its name is derived from its frequent companion, the
    monarch butterfly, which dines on its clusters of five curved and five
    upright petals. This plant also is called **pleurisy root** because Native
    Americans chewed its roots to alleviate the lung condition we now
    know as pleurisy.

    Walk on a wooden boardwalk that crosses a man-made pond.
    Although this body of water is named Turtle Pond because of the sev-
    eral painted turtles that live here, you are more apt to spot **Canada geese**
    than turtles. These large, web-footed birds are easy to identify because
    they have black heads and necks interrupted by a thick white band
    underneath the chin. Canada geese are monogamous and do not allow
    any deviation from their strict moral code. If a couple leaves the flock
    and the male returns without his mate, the other geese will chase him
    away.

2. Fork left onto the Shad Trail, so named because of the shadbushes
    growing under large oak and sassafras trees at the start of the trail.

    Shadbush got its name from a coincidence of timing. In May shadfish
    migrate upstream to spawn, and at the same time the shadbush's fra-
    grant white flowers begin to bloom. Shadbush is also called **Juneberry**
    because its flower clusters turn into reddish purple berries in June. This
    trail could also be named the Blueberry Trail because of the number of
    bushes that line the path.

3. The Shad Trail leads to an inlet of Sengekontacket Pond called Majors Cove.

Once you have reached the shore, turn right and follow the coast through a marshy area.

This marshland is the main reason why large numbers of shorebirds summer on Felix Neck. **Cordgrass** and **salt marsh hay** provide food and shelter for both finfish and shellfish, which in turn draw many varieties of shorebirds. As you walk along the beach you'll find numerous shells, some cracked and some with beak holes, that have been discarded by our feathered friends.

Interspersed among the cordgrass grows **common glasswort**, distinguished by its cactuslike branches. A favorite of ducks and geese, glasswort was also popular with early settlers, who used its stems for making pickles and sprinkled its branch tips on salads to add a salty flavor.

Unless the tide is very high, you can continue walking along the water's edge as the shoreline bends in an easterly direction. If high water prevents you from walking along the shore, take your next right onto the Beach Trail and pick up the directions at No. 6. If remaining next to the pond, you'll spot Beach Road and the Joseph Sylvia State Beach, which separate Sengekontacket Pond from Vineyard Sound.

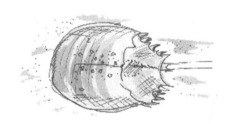

Horseshoe crab

The water in Sengekontacket Pond is seeded for scallops and clams. During low tide you'll often see clammers raking up quahogs or digging for steamers. As you stroll along the shore, watch for clam, mussel, whelk, and scallop shells. You may also find the molt of a **horseshoe crab**. The molt, which looks like a dead horseshoe crab, is actually its cast-off shell—the crab outgrew its covering in the same way a ten-year-old's jacket fits for only one season. If you are not squeamish, pick up this strange-looking arthropod and look for the little slit that the crab used as an escape hatch. Horseshoe crabs, like ticks, are arachnids, prehistoric fauna that have been around for thousands of years.

If you venture into the water, you may see **green crabs** with flat oval shells and **spider crabs** with spiny circular bodies. Check the bottom for **mud snails**, the pond's sanitary engineers. They clean the water by eating decayed organic matter that has settled on the pond floor.

4. Continue walking along this northern tip of the sanctuary until you see a wide opening, which is the continuation of the Yellow Trail. Turn right.

5. At the next intersection, turn right remaining on the Yellow Trail.

6. Go around another man-made body of water named Elizabeth's Pond and turn left onto the Red Trail.

This path travels through a pitch pine forest with an undercover of bayberry and huckleberry bushes. You'll notice that the trees and bushes are smaller and more deformed here than in the other areas of Felix Neck. Because this land is higher and less protected, its vegetation is continually bombarded by wind and salt spray.

This route skirts the pond. The path next to the water appears to be a favorite dumping ground, where birds discard shells after devouring the mollusks inside. You may find a whelk shell, decorated with beak holes, to take home as a souvenir.

Across the water lies Sarson's Island, a nesting ground for **double-crested cormorants**. These birds are easy to spot because their dark color and long necks easily distinguish them from the light-colored sea gull. You often will see them sunning on a rock or piece of land. Unlike most water fowl, cormorants don't produce the oil that enables water to run off their feathers, so they are forced to spend much of their time drying their wings.

American oystercatchers, an endangered species that has been protected, now occupy the southern half of the island. Their bright-red beaks and black-and-white bodies make them easy to spot.

7. At the junction of the Red and Orange Trails, hook a left onto the Orange Trail and walk through the marsh toward the water.

Great blue herons, long-legged, grayish blue wading birds with pointed bills and long necks, frequently visit this area.

8. Proceed through this marshy section, circling back to rejoin the trail.

9. At the junction of the Red and Orange Trails, bear left onto the Orange Trail.

10. Remain on the Orange Trail until you come to a right turn which leads to the Waterfowl Pond and the observation blind. Turn right, cross the bridge, and enter the small cabin. A poster with pictures and names of ducks and other waterfowl that frequent Felix Neck hangs on the wall.

11. From the observation blind, turn right and follow the shore of the pond. The stone bench provides a convenient stop to rest and watch ducks paddle by.

12. Follow the path to the dirt road. Turn left on the road, to head back to the parking lot.

    If after leaving the observation blind you are interested in further investigation of the salt marsh, remain on the dirt road until you come to the junction of the Jessica Hancock Memorial Trail (Green Trail). Turn left. This short loop runs next to the marsh.

    To return to the parking lot from the Hancock Trail, turn left onto the Orange Trail.

CHAPTER NINETEEN

Mytoi—East Beach

Who would expect a Japanese-style garden to be tucked away on Chappaquiddick? Mytoi grew from an unusual bequest, which stipulated the land be used to create a serene sanctuary filled with unusual plantings, brooks, benches, and bridges. Across Dike Road a rustic trail winds through woods that border a salt marsh.

East Beach, located at the end of Dike Road, offers isolation, beauty, and fine white sand.

Directions: From the Chappaquiddick ferry, travel 2.5 miles on Chappaquiddick Road. When the road bends sharply to the right, continue straight onto unpaved Dike Road. Proceed 0.5 mile to Mytoi. The parking lot and bike rack are on the left, just past the reservation.

To reach Dike Bridge and East Beach from Mytoi, continue 0.2 mile farther down the road. A parking lot and bike rack are located just before the bridge.

Distance: 0.3 mile around the garden; 0.4 mile through the woods to the salt marsh.

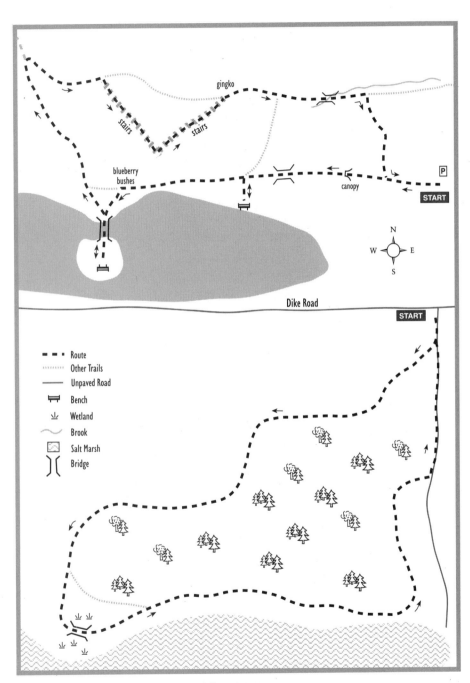

MYTOI

Difficulty: Easy.

Restrooms: At the east end of the Mytoi parking lot and also next to the gate-house at Dike Bridge.

Food and drink: Chappy General Store, located 2.2 miles from the Chappy Ferry and 0.3 mile from Dike Road; water fountain just beyond the entrance to Mytoi.

Fees: The entrance fee for East Beach is $3. Children under twelve and members of the Trustees of Reservations are free.

Background: In 1958 Mary Wakeman donated the Mytoi property to the Trustees of Reservations, a nonprofit conservation organization. Her gift included this three-and-a-half-acre garden and ten acres of pine forest across the road. The garden contains native and exotic plants and trees which have been chosen to maintain visual interest throughout the year. Witch hazel blooms in February and March. In spring Mytoi is awash with color from the blossoms of wild roses, rhododendrons, azaleas, daffodils, primrose, lady's slippers, and dogwood and stewartia trees. In summer the purple petals of the Japanese iris decorate the pond. In autumn look for white blossoms decorating the rare Franklinia tree.

THE ROUTE

1.   Enter Mytoi under the arch built from tree trunks and limbs. On the left the trail passes rhododendron bushes, a cluster of hay-scented ferns, and four varieties of birch saplings—Himalayan, paper, European river, and heritage.

     Passing through a wooden structure that serves to formally welcome you to the garden, you then walk along a stone path, passing a bench on the left. The bench is one of many donated by Chappaquiddick residents. Next to the bench stands an unusual-looking tree called **thread-needle cypress**.

2.   After crossing a tiny stone bridge, turn left onto a path that ends at a rock garden adorned with a variety of ground covers. Another bench facing the pond encourages quiet contemplation.

3.   Returning to the main path, continue to the pond.

     On the left side of the path sits a tiny **Japanese maple** tree with feathery, russet-colored leaves. It provides a marked contrast in size, color, and leaf texture to its neighbor, the **tamarack** tree, which looks like an ever-green, with needles sprouting in clusters on the tops of its branches. But it doesn't act like an evergreen—the tamarack sheds its needles in the fall.

Highbush blueberries overlook the pond. Across the path stand a cluster of cultivated blueberry bushes whose berries are twice the size of the wild ones. In July the purple blooms at the edge of the pond belong

Mytoi offers a peaceful stop for weary hikers.

to the **Japanese iris**. In August **pickerel** decorate the pond with their purple flowers.

4.   Turn left to cross a footbridge onto the small island.

Wooden benches allow you to sit, watch, and listen to the inhabitants of the pond. On the water you'll see **whirligig beetles** swimming in their never-ending circles, while **water striders** are busily jumping from spot to spot. See if you can find **goldfish** and **koi** or painted and snapping turtles. Bright-yellow markings on the head and neck of the **painted turtle** distinguish it from the **snapping turtle**. The croaking frogs blend so well with the background that you are more likely to hear than see them.

5. Return to the path and turn left. Proceed up the stairs to the upper trail, passing a garden of ground covers including cotoneaster, juniper, and bearberry.

6. A **holly** tree with dark-green waxy leaves stands on your left before the right turn onto another set of stairs which leads to an overview of the garden.

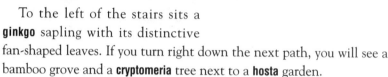

Holly

7. Descend to the other side of the hill and turn right.

    To the left of the stairs sits a **ginkgo** sapling with its distinctive fan-shaped leaves. If you turn right down the next path, you will see a bamboo grove and a **cryptomeria** tree next to a **hosta** garden.

8. Back on the main trail, cross the bridge.

    On the left a cluster of **azalea** bushes produce colorful blooms in May. On the right stands an **English beech** tree with its distinctive drooping branches.

    Continue to the brook and tiny waterfall. They were created by first excavating earth to form the small pond and then digging channels to direct the flow of water from the well near the parking lot. The excavated soil was used to build the hills that surround the garden.

9. Turn right to head back to the entrance path.

10. Turn left to leave this section of Mytoi.

11. To walk through an environment that offers a marked contrast to this manicured garden, and to view wildlife around the salt marsh, exit from the parking lot and cross Dike Road.

12. Head down the dirt road and take the first right. The trail curves right and then bends left as it follows an inlet from Poucha Pond.

13. At the fork bear right onto a side path for an unobstructed view of the birds and wildlife that inhabit the salt marsh.

You may spot otters scampering through the high grass, called **phragmites**, or great blue herons, snowy egrets, and black-and-white American oystercatchers standing in the marsh.

14.   Bear right to continue on the main trail.

15.   Turn left onto the dirt road to return to the parking lot.

East Beach

To access East Beach, you now can cross Dike Bridge (it reopened in 1995). Tourists continue to flock here, thirty years after Senator Edward Kennedy's car containing passenger Mary Jo Kopechne, went off the bridge and sank in Poucha Pond. But most of these sightseers are not aware that a world-class beach lies on the opposite side of the bridge. For more than a decade after the accident the bridge had not been passable, and East Beach was accessible only by paying a hefty fee to navigate a four-wheel-drive vehicle 2 miles from Wasque Reservation.

If after crossing Dike Bridge you turn right and proceed 1.5 miles, you will enter Wasque Reservation. If you turn left at East Beach, you will head toward Cape Poge Wildlife Refuge. This isolated barrier beach travels north for 3 miles. On the right lies the Muskeget Channel in Nantucket Sound and on the left Cape Poge Bay.

A variety of shorebirds, including osprey, oystercatchers, and least and common terns, feed and nest in this area.

Among the vegetation that grows in this sandy soil is **sea rocket**, a member of the mustard family, with large seed pods and fleshy leaves that taste like horseradish. **Eel grass**, which produces flowers only in saltwater, grows near the marsh. The beach-loving *Rosa rugosa* decorates the dunes with its pink blossoms in the spring and shiny red rose hips in the summer and fall.

You may spot fishermen casting on the outer shores of the refuge or boats carrying shell fishermen seeking scallops in the warm shallow water of Cape Poge Bay. Many varieties of gulls line the shore and plunge from the sky, competing with the fishermen for the abundant fish.

CHAPTER TWENTY

Wasque Reservation

If you travel as far southeast as you can go on Chappaquiddick, you'll land at Wasque (pronounced *Way-skwee*) Reservation. Here miles of secluded barrier beach separate Wasque's southern tip from the Atlantic Ocean's dynamic surf, with waves to daunt the most intrepid bodysurfer. Calm Katama Bay, a haven for windsurfers and clammers, lies on the west side of the reservation. Poucha Pond and Muskeget Channel bound Wasque on the east. One of the properties owned by the Trustees of Reservations, Wasque offers biking, hiking, swimming, picnicking, and bird-watching within its 200 acres.

Directions: After disembarking from the ferry, follow the paved road for 4.5 miles. When the pavement turns to sand, continue for 0.7 mile. If you have a mountain or hybrid bike and can navigate this sandy section, you will avoid the possibility of facing a "filled to capacity" parking lot.

Distance: 3 miles.

Difficulty: Easy.

Fees: Biking will eliminate the $3 car entrance fee; however, you will have to pay $3 per person to enter. Members of the Trustees of Reservations and children under fifteen are admitted free.

Restrooms: Located at the entrance, at the beach parking lot, and at the parking lot near Wasque Point.

Food and drink: Water pumps are located at both ends of the main parking lot. Wasque is a great place for picnicking, with lots of tables overlooking the water.

Background: Wasque Reservation was formed about 15,000 years ago. Rivers of water flowed off a 10,000-foot glacier and deposited sand and gravel picked up as the glacier inched southward. This accumulation of sand and gravel formed the outwash plain that composes the south side of the island.

Once you reach Wasque and look west toward Edgartown, you'll discover that Chappaquiddick is not really an island but a peninsula. Chappaquiddick has been an island only ten times in the last two hundred years, when violent storms created a breach in the barrier beach connecting to Edgartown. Then, no vehicles could travel the 3-mile stretch from Edgartown's South Beach to Wasque Point, the premier bluefishing spot on Martha's Vineyard.

If you travel north from Wasque Point, you will enter Cape Poge Wildlife Refuge, a 509-acre property also owned by the Trustees of Reservations. Wasque and Cape Poge are two of the many Massachusetts properties owned and operated by the Trustees, the oldest land trust in the world. This non-profit organization preserves properties of exceptional scenic, historic, and ecological value. Other Trustees of Reservations properties on Martha's Vineyard are Long Point, Mytoi, and Menemsha Hills Reservations.

To reach Cape Poge, plan on hiking for five hours. One alternative is to hitch a ride on one of the four-wheel-drive vehicles heading to secluded spots for sunning, fishing, and swimming. Driving on this sandy beach not only requires skill and practice but also a pricey permit, which can be purchased from the Trustees. Another possibility is to explore Cape Poge via dune buggy on one of the Trustees' popular three-hour natural history tours.

The Cape Poge barrier beach was formed differently from other Vineyard barrier beaches. South-facing beaches were formed when ocean currents carried sand and debris from the western end of the Vineyard. At Cape Poge, which faces east, the ocean tides, currents, and winds pulled glacial deposits from the ocean floor and created a sandbar that increased in height until it rose above sea level. The sandbar reduced the size and height of the waves that pounded the beach, allowing the barrier beach to grow to its present size.

THE ROUTE

1. Begin at the trailhead east of the gatehouse and just behind a picnic bench. Follow the wide, pine-needle-covered trail (great for biking) as it runs through a pine forest and oak woodland. The trail enters a meadow and borders Poucha Pond. Remain on the trail as it crosses a dirt road and becomes a wood-chipped trail that cuts across sandplain grassland, which purposely has been cut to maintain this habitat.

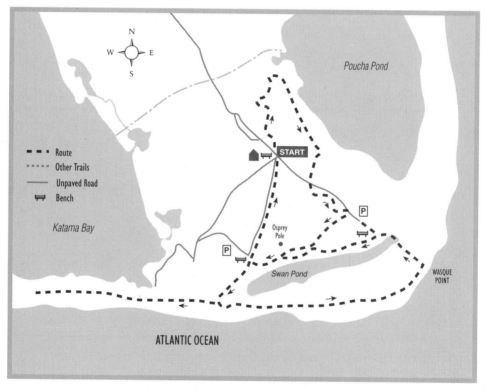

𝕏𝕏 WASQUE RESERVATION

Stop for a minute in this scrubby heathland to appreciate the water views and investigate the flora. In the spring look for **trailing arbutus**, which produces small clusters of pink or white flowers that give off a fragrant, sweet smell. If you are visiting in late summer and fall, the heathland is dotted with **New York asters**, small lavender flowers with bright yellow centers.

2. The trail enters a forest of small pitch pine trees. After emerging, turn right at the T intersection, heading toward Swan Pond.

3. Bear right at the fork.

On the right, a high pole houses eaglelike **osprey**, who often sit on their perch and scan the water for fish.

4. Continue straight as the path merges and widens, running parallel to Swan Pond.

As befits its name, Swan Pond often boasts a couple of **swans.** It's rare to see just one swan, as they usually travel in pairs. In late spring and summer you may see a couple with their cygnets paddling behind in a straight line. If the cygnets are under a year old, they will be covered with grayish brown down. Female swans lay their eggs in large nests built with water plants and line them with the down from their bodies. Swans feed on seeds and roots of water plants, along with shellfish and worms.

Swan Pond previously connected Poucha Pond on the east, with Katama Bay on the west. However, each year the pond diminishes in size.

5. Bear left on the path heading toward the boardwalk. A bench provides a rest stop, if necessary, before you hike down the boardwalk to the beach.

The long wooden ramp guarantees that visitors will not stray into the fragile dune area. In order to stabilize the dunes, environmentalists encourage the growth of beach grass. Its strong root system helps to anchor the dune and prevent erosion. Notice that **beach grass**, which can withstand a harsh, windy, and salty environment, is the only vegetation growing on the steep seaward side of the dunes. The softer, more sloping inland, or protected side, of the dune hosts a variety of plants. Look for the delicate blue-gray **dusty miller,** which produces small yellow flowers in the summer. Its fuzzy, dusty-looking protective covering helps the plant conserve water so that it can grow in arid conditions. You may also spot **seaside goldenrod**, another plant that has adapted to this harsh environment. In the fall it decorates the sand with clusters of bright yellow flowers.

6. Upon reaching the beach you have a choice: you can turn right onto the 2-mile barrier beach separating the ocean and Katama Bay or turn left toward Wasque Point.

    The section of sand bordering Katama Bay is a good example of up-island's loss becoming down-island's gain. Although erosion annually

Seaside goldenrod

Dusty miller

sweeps away about 8 feet of the Vineyard's southern shoreline, strong easterly currents have carried the sand from up-island cliffs and beaches to create this barrier beach.

You may spot **sandpipers**, tiny birds with long bills who prefer isolated beaches, where they can peacefully chase each receding wave in their quest for sand fleas. And the **sand fleas**, or "beach hoppers," emerge from their minuscule holes in the wet sand with their own mission—to find and gobble up plankton before the next wave rolls in.

If you walk west toward Katama Bay, be aware of the tern nesting areas. **Least terns**, with their long, pointed wings, resemble gulls but have thinner bodies and bills. If you spot terns circling noisily above your head, you're probably too close to their nesting area. Head quickly toward the water before the mother tern mounts an attack.

7. If you turn left toward **Wasque Point** and stroll for twenty minutes, you will land at the spot where fishermen gather to cast for "big blues."

Bluefish and bass abound at Wasque Point due to the convergence of currents flowing toward the east and south. Because of these strong currents, swimming is prohibited here.

Cape Poge Wildlife Refuge lies 2 miles beyond Wasque Point. Thousands of sea- and shorebirds, including **ospreys, oystercatchers**, and **piping plovers**, seek Cape Poge's isolated location to nest, feed, and rest. Fishermen favor Cape Poge because the surf-casting off the refuge's outer shores is among the best on the Atlantic coast.

8. Upon reaching Wasque Point, turn left onto the wooden boardwalk.

9. After climbing the stairs, turn left onto the trail, passing the reservation's premier picnic spot, with many tables and benches in addition to a great view. This section of the trail runs adjacent to Swan Pond before it converges with the path you walked earlier.

10. At the boardwalk turn right onto the access road that returns to the gatehouse and trailhead.

CHAPTER TWENTY-ONE

Camp Meeting Grounds

Now the liveliest island town, with the most nightclubs and fast-food shops, ironically Oak Bluffs first existed as a place to pray, not play. In 1835 members of the Methodist church began meeting in what was then known as Cottage City. Each August a small group pitched their tents on the campground, relaxed during the day, and attended nightly prayer meetings. To preserve their tightly-knit community with the church as its central focus, the Camp Meeting Association members built Victorian-era brightly colored homes, adorned with ornate trim, around the Tabernacle. Residents have conscientiously preserved these quaint cottages so visitors to the Camp Meeting Grounds can view architecture as it was a hundred years ago.

Directions: Begin where New York Avenue borders Oak Bluffs Harbor.

Distance: 1.3 miles.

Difficulty: Easy walking.

Restrooms: Public toilets are located next to the Steamship Authority terminal at the end of Lake Street.

Food and drink: Circuit Avenue, which flanks the east side of the Camp Meeting Grounds, offers a wide variety of shops and restaurants.

Fees: Cottage Museum, Flying Horses carousel.

Background: An interesting speculation is whether Martha's Vineyard would have developed as a popular resort if Oak Bluffs had not been the site of religious meetings. It is hard to believe that a beautiful island located near New York and Boston would remain a farming and fishing community. But it took the religious fervor of the island's summer visitors to jump-start the habit of annual pilgrimages to Cottage City, Oak Bluffs' name during its formative years.

This resurgence of religion began in the early nineteenth century, when proponents of the Methodist movement, who preached personal salvation, were vigorously seeking converts. These preachers found outdoor camp meetings, which encouraged soul-searching and emotionalism, to be well suited for this type of proselytizing. One of these preachers, Jeremiah Pease of Edgartown, sought a remote, undeveloped area near the seashore for a meeting place. He found a secluded spot under a large grove of oaks near Squash Meadow Pond. In the summer of 1835 the Methodists pitched their tents and established the Martha's Vineyard Camp Meeting. They called the area, now known as Trinity Park, Wesleyan Grove.

For many summers church groups from Providence, New Bedford, Boston, and Nantucket attended meetings held under tall oak trees. Worshippers sat on rough benches and slept in small tents. As the number of families grew, the tents became larger. In a spirit of true togetherness, some congregations constructed huge tents, which they partitioned down the middle to separate the sexes.

The congregants found their annual camp meetings so pleasurable that they began to arrive earlier and remain later. Families staying for longer and longer periods of time soon found the tents to be inadequate. By the 1860s small Victorian-style cottages were built as close together as the tents they replaced. By 1880, 315 cottages had been built. The cottages were small and boxlike, but owners individualized their homes by adding wooden filigree decoration. Although many of the houses have been remodeled and enlarged, their gingerbread trim and colorful facades continue to reflect the festive spirit of their former occupants.

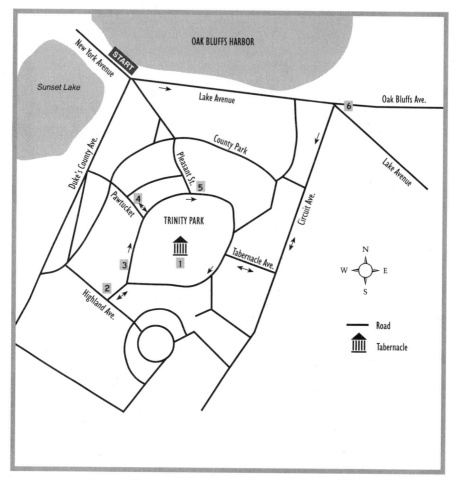

🚶🚶 CAMP MEETING GROUNDS

THE ROUTE

1. Begin on New York Avenue, with the harbor on the left and Sunset Lake on the right.

   Originally Sunset Lake and Oak Bluffs Harbor were one body of water, which was called Squash Meadow Pond. When the harbor and channel were dredged, Squash Meadow became a separate pond. After the causeway was built between the pond and harbor, it further defined the separation.

With your back to the harbor, go left (east). On your right is the **Wesley Hotel**, an example of the grand wooden hotels with large, inviting verandas that were popular a hundred years ago. Unfortunately, these structures often burned down. Although a fire once destroyed the Wesley, it was rebuilt and today is the sole survivor of the island's Victorian-era hotels.

2.   Turn right onto Circuit Avenue, walking past all the shops and restaurants.

3.   Turn right onto a tiny side street named Tabernacle Avenue (a store, the Secret Garden, sits on the corner). After you turn you'll see a sign announcing the entrance to the Martha's Vineyard Camp Meeting Grounds.

4.   Once you reach Trinity Park, distinguished by the Tabernacle in the center, turn left.

   In 1879 Camp Meeting participants built the **Tabernacle** (1 on the map) so that their expanding population would have a suitable place to hold services. This unusual iron structure replaced a one-ton tent that had taken the place of the oak-tree-grove meeting spot. The Tabernacle seats more than three thousand people and now is used for interdenominational services and musical events.

5.   Circle around the Tabernacle until you find the structure on the left that houses the Camp Meeting Association office. Here you can obtain a schedule of events that take place in the Tabernacle.

6.   Turn left on the main walkway as it veers away from the Tabernacle.

   On the right corner the **Cottage Museum** (2) allows the curious to inspect the inside of a cottage and examine its furnishings. The museum is open from 10:00 A.M. to 4:00 P.M., Monday through Saturday. The entrance fee is $1.

7.   Head back toward the Tabernacle and proceed down the walkway to the left of the Tabernacle.

   After passing several houses, you'll come to a large home numbered 10 and named the Ark (3). This home, the largest and fanciest of that time, cost $3,500 to build. It belonged to William Sprague, the governor of Rhode Island during the Civil War.

   In 1860 there were 500 tents in this area. Now there are 315 cottages, which were constructed between 1862 and 1880, each with a front porch that faces the Tabernacle. If you look above the front door you'll find the year the cottage was built. Most of these original houses contained only four rooms—two bedrooms upstairs and a living room and bedroom downstairs. There was no need for a kitchen or bathroom because there was no plumbing. The "cottagers" cooked in cook tents and used outhouses located near the dwellings.

During your walk, you'll notice that most of the cottages have the same general design: high-peaked roofs, wide front porches, and a balcony over the front door. The balcony was not just a decorative addition. It allowed more air to enter the hot, stuffy second floor and it provided access for the beds and bureaus that couldn't be carried up the narrow stairway. To individualize each cottage, the owner often used the newly invented jigsaw to cut elaborate filigree work which he painted with bright colors.

8.   Turn left on Pawtucket Avenue.

The name of the second house on the right is Tall Timbers (4). Its name refers to the one-piece pine boards that start at the ground floor and travel up to its third story.

9.   Return to the main walkway.

Another unusual sight (5) is on the corner of Pleasant Street—a lot with flowers, bushes, and trees but no cottages. Three homes once stood on this land, but all were bought by the resident living in the house on the left, who gardens this plot.

Although owners have purchased their cottages, the land is owned by the Martha's Vineyard Camp Meeting Gounds Association, which issues annual leases to the purchasers. The association directors then have the option of not renewing the leases of undesirable tenants.

Continue to walk around the campground and look at these colorful dwellings, representative of Carpenter Gothic architecture. These homes are literally spotlighted during **Illumination Night**, which occurs on a Wednesday night in either the second or third week in August. The date varies and is not advertised until the last minute, in order to minimize the crowds, which are still huge. Illumination Night began in 1869 as an annual celebration of the end-of-summer religious meetings. The recent addition of a sing-along band concert has made this unique event even more festive. Cottage owners illuminate their dwelling with ornate, colorful, Japanese-style lanterns, trying to outdo their neighbors in the number and variety of lights. Throngs of viewers parade by on the sidewalks, while the cottage owners and their friends party on front porches and gaze at the spectators strolling by.

10. After walking around the campground, return to Tabernacle Avenue and proceed out to Circuit Avenue.

11. Turn left.

Walk on the right side of the street if you are looking for food or drink: Mad Martha's for ice cream, Cozy's for sandwiches and ice cream, Subway for grinders (submarine sandwiches), and Giordano's, located on the corner of Circuit Avenue across from the information booth, for delicious pizza that you can eat in or take out.

Across from Giordano's, nestled on the wedge between Oak Bluffs and Lake Avenues, rests the oldest operating platform carousel in the country. The **Flying Horses** (6), built in 1876, is registered as a National Historical Landmark. Riders on the original wooden horses continue the tradition of reaching for the brass ring in order to win a free ride. The carousel is open daily from 1:00 P.M. to 9:00 P.M. from May to November.

12. To return to your starting point, go west on Lake Avenue.

CHAPTER TWENTY-TWO

Trade Wind Fields Preserve

Take a wide, grassy airfield and surround it by woods and a scenic golf course. What do you get? A paradise for dogs and dog walkers. Dogs love the open grassland for chasing balls and each other. Walkers are grateful for the wide, level paths that snake through woodlands and border the Farm Neck Golf Club. Owners have trained their dogs to wait patiently as they stop to pick the bountiful blueberries and huckleberries from the bushes that line the trail.

Directions: The preserve sits on County Road in Oak Bluffs, 2 miles north of the intersection with the Edgartown–Vineyard Haven Road and 0.25 mile south of the intersection with Wing Road. The access road is one-way and can be reached by traveling 0.2 mile on Wing Road and turning right on Pheasant Lane. At the T intersection, turn left onto Meadow Way. Follow Meadow Way until it ends at Trade Wind Road. Turn right and continue 0.2 mile to the entrance and parking lot on the right.

Distance: 1.3 miles; 3 miles with the visit to Farm Pond.

Difficulty: Easy.

Background: Owned and maintained by the Martha's Vineyard Land Bank Commission, Trade Wind Fields continues to be used as a grass-strip airport (pilots must have a "permission to land" slip issued by the Land Bank). For decades the land has been mowed and rolled to ensure a smooth landing. As a result, half of the 72-acre preserve has remained sandplain grassland. This habitat was formed when sand and gravel flowed off the melting glacier and formed much of Martha's Vineyard. Most of the sandplain, left unattended, became woodland (the state forest is a good example). Sandplain soil is porous and supports only drought-resistant plants. Nantucket shadbush, bushy rock rose, and sandplain blue-eyed grass are several rare species that have adapted to this environment.

THE ROUTE

1. Head out of the parking lot and turn left. The Red Trail circles the runway, while the Blue Trail runs through the woods.

2. Go straight on the wide, open path until you spot a wooden post topped with a red blaze. At this intersection of the Red and Blue Trails, turn left onto the Blue Trail. A blue Land Bank marker is nailed to a tree a few hundred feet ahead on the left.

    The trail first passes through a meadow before it heads into a pine forest. The meadow is host to a wide variety of wildflowers. In August white blooms from **pearly everlasting** dot the field. Its name describes its naturally dry blooms, which have a papery texture and last much longer than other flowers. Later in the month, pearly everlasting is joined by **golden asters,** whose small, bright-yellow flowers form clusters at the end of their branches. **Chicory,** another plant that thrives in dry places, adds a touch of blue to the meadow. Its common name, ragged sailor, refers to the tendency of its blue blossoms, which last only twenty-four hours, to become more bedraggled as the day progresses.

    Upon entering the forest, the path, cushioned with pine needles, passes oak saplings and an abundance of blueberry and huckleberry bushes. Before you start picking, check to make sure there is no poison ivy growing near the bushes. (Green shiny leaves in groups of three that grow at ground level or at bush height.)

3. If you wish to visit Farm Pond and extend your walk 0.8 mile each way, turn left on the path that leads first to the Oak Bluffs Elementary School and then to Farm Pond, another property owned by the Land Bank. If you prefer to remain in Trade Wind Fields, skip to No. 9.

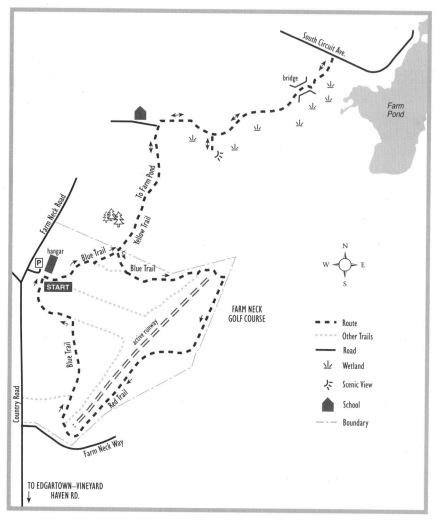

👣👣 TRADE WIND FIELDS PRESERVE

4.   Proceed straight on the path with yellow markers to the school access road. Just before you reach the school, the Yellow Trail crosses a dirt road. Turn right and immediately look for a path that runs through the woods parallel to the school. The path passes the basketball court and playground. Look for the yellow markers.

5.   Follow the path as it crosses wetlands. A spur on the right leads to a boardwalk that extends into the marsh.

6.   Continue another 0.25 mile to Farm Pond.

During the summer Farm Pond has two very visible visitors—metal sea serpent sculptures of Vanessa and her child perched in the middle of the pond.

7. The trail meets South Circuit Avenue. If you wish to continue another 0.5 mile to explore the Beach Road section of Farm Pond Preserve, turn right on South Circuit Avenue. Take your first left on Katama Avenue and first right onto Seaview Road. Follow to Beach Road. Turn right on Beach Road to Farm Pond Preserve.

8. To return, retrace your route.

9. To find the trail back to Trade Winds from the Oak Bluffs Elementary School, turn right onto the dirt road and then take an immediate left. A large boulder marks the entrance to the path to the airfield.

10. Remain on the path for about 0.3 mile and turn left onto the trail to continue your loop around the runway.

11. Turn left again to resume walking on the Blue Trail.

12. Follow the trail as it leaves the woods and follows the runway. Turn left. Although the field does not receive much air traffic, be alert for the occasional plane landing or taking off.

13. Turn right at the road that runs between the Farm Neck Golf Club and the airfield. Don't miss the fields of multicolored wildflowers growing amidst sand traps and manicured putting greens.

14. Follow the dirt road as it re-enters the grassland habitat, joins the Red Trail, and borders the runway. Blueberry bushes dot the grassland.

    As you walk, you may hear the *thwunk* of tennis rackets hitting balls on the tennis courts that belong to the golf course.

    The bright orange flower that adorns the field in August is called **butterfly weed**. It is also called pleurisy root because Native Americans chewed on its root to alleviate the condition we now know as pleurisy. Watch for the monarch butterfly, which often dines on its petals. **Queen Anne's lace** is the tall white flower that looks like its petals are made of lace.

15. At the intersection with the Blue Trail turn left to enter a pine forest. Again, a bounty of blueberries grow alongside the trail.

16. After leaving the forest, turn left onto the runway path. Follow the path as it loops around the western end of the field and returns to the parking lot. Landing blocks that may or may not hold a plane sit on the field to the left of the trail.

CHAPTER TWENTY-THREE

Christiantown—
Christiantown Woods Preserve

In Christiantown, the first Christian Indian village on the island, a quaint little chapel sits adjacent to an old Indian graveyard dotted with plain stone markers. Behind the chapel lies Christiantown Woods, where a short trail winds around remnants of farms that occupied the land hundreds of years ago.

Directions: Traveling west on State Road in West Tisbury, turn right onto Indian Hill Road (the next right after Upper Lambert's Cove Road). Proceed 0.5 mile and turn right onto Christiantown Road. (There may not be a street sign, but there is a Private Road sign.) Continue for 0.6 mile on this dirt road to the parking lot on the left.

Distance: 0.5 mile.

Difficulty: Easy.

Food and drink: Up-Island Cronig's Market and Biga Bakery deli on the left side of Indian Hill Road, just after the turn from State Road.

Background: In 1659 Sachem Josias Keteanummin donated land to be used as a settlement for Indian converts to Christianity. Later this square-mile plot was named Christiantown.

THE ROUTE

1.   Begin at the little chapel on the left, which is open only on Sundays. It contains a tiny altar and six pews.

Erected in 1829, the **Christiantown Chapel** replaced the original house of worship. It also is called the **Mayhew Chapel**, after Reverend Thomas Mayhew Jr., the son of Thomas Mayhew, one of the island's original settlers. Reverend Mayhew was instrumental in converting the Wampanoag tribe to Christianity.

2.   Climb the small hill across the road from the chapel to the **Indian Burial Ground**.

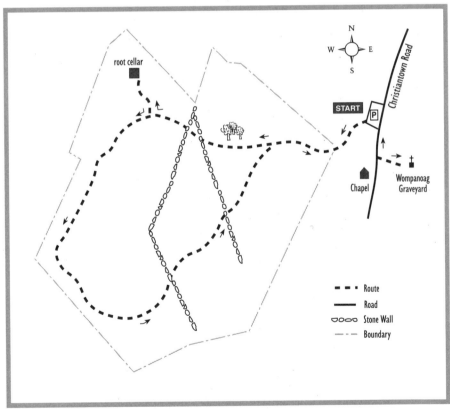

🥾🥾 CHRISTIANTOWN WOODS PRESERVE

The Mayhew Chapel in Christiantown Woods Preserve.

This little cemetery was created by Sachem Keteanummin for the Wampanoag converts to Christianity. The smooth fieldstone grave markers reveal no information about who is buried below.

3. Return to the road and turn right, heading back toward the parking lot and Christiantown Woods Preserve.

4. At the parking lot, turn left to enter Christiantown Woods.

The trees here are much taller than in other Vineyard forests. Their height reflects the length of time that has passed since the land was farmed.

5. Turn right onto the trail that loops through the woodland.

The woods are filled with **pignut hickory** trees, a variety not common to the island. The pignut hickory usually has five pointed, finely toothed leaflets and in autumn bears round, hard-shelled nuts. These nuts grow in husks that split into four parts when broken.

6. Bear right at the fork.

7. Turn right onto a side trail for the opportunity to rest on "Reclining Rock" (my name for the long, low glacial erratic [a boulder dropped here when the last glacier receded] that resembles a lounge chair).

8. Return to the trail and take the next right to visit an old root cellar, formerly a basement in a sheep farmer's home two hundred years ago.

   There were no woods then, as the settlers clearcut the land to use the trees for fuel and shelter. The open fields were defined by the now crumbling stone wall, built to contain animals. This land reverted back to woods when farming ceased being profitable.

9. Return to the main trail and continue the loop. At the junction turn right to return to the parking area.

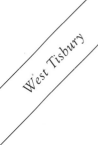

CHAPTER TWENTY-FOUR

Cedar Tree Neck Wildlife Sanctuary

One of my favorite hiking spots on Martha's Vineyard is Cedar Tree Neck. I love its variety of terrain and spectacular views. Three separate trails provide a microcosm of the Vineyard's natural features as they run through woods, across streams, by ponds, and along a beach. The high point of the hike is the Brown Trail, which loops around a bluff with a sequence of vistas of Vineyard Sound and the Elizabeth Islands. As a counterpoint to all this beauty, a sphagnum bog provides a smelly diversion.

Directions: Traveling west on State Road in West Tisbury, turn right on Indian Hill Road (just past the turn to lower Lambert's Cove Road). Follow Indian Hill Road for 1.3 miles. Turn right on Obed Daggett Road. Keep your eye out for the sanctuary signs as you remain on this dirt road for 1 mile.

Distance: 2.8 miles.

Difficulty: Moderate; some steep sections on the White Trail.

Food and drink: Up-Island Cronig's Market and Biga Bakery deli, at the intersection of State and Indian Hill Roads.

Background: Cedar Tree Neck Sanctuary was acquired through a cooperative fund-raising campaign by the Sheriff's Meadow Foundation, a land conservation organization, and the Massachusetts Audubon Society. Sheriff's Meadow tries to protect natural areas as living museums and prohibits swimming and picnicking on all their properties.

THE ROUTE

Do be careful of poison ivy in and around the trail (look for three shiny, dark-green leaflets). If you think you may have rubbed against the plant, scrub the area with soap and water upon your return.

1. Facing the sanctuary from the parking lot, head to the left onto the White Trail.

   After entering the white-blazed trail, look to the left for a cluster of **sassafras** trees on both sides of the path. Watch for trees with three different shapes of leaves: one a simple oval shape, another with two lobes that look like a mitten, and a third that has three lobes. Island settlers hollowed out sassafras trees to use as canoes and then boiled the roots and bark for tea. You'll discover sassafras trees throughout the sanctuary.

Sassafras

   Continue walking past the Purple Trail marker on the right. Look to your left for a forest of **red pine** trees, which have flexible needlelike leaves hanging in clusters of two. Pine trees often form a canopy that prevents light from reaching the ground, so very few plants grow on the floor of a pine forest.

2. Remain on the White Trail past the Yellow Trail marker on the right. Continue straight at the junction where there is a spur to the White Trail.

   The trail ascends and descends for about a 0.5 mile before it reaches a sphagnum bog. Just before the bog is a grove of sassafras trees and a clump of **Massachusetts ferns**. This species of fern thrives in swampy areas. One of the distinguishing characteristics of the Massachusetts fern is the downward slant of its lowest pair of leaflets.

At the bog, rest for a moment on the benches. Soon you will smell fumes emanating from the bog. This characteristic odor comes from the release of sulfur from waterlogged soil.

The **sphagnum bog** began as a glacial excavation where water collected. Since water cannot flow out of this low-lying area and there are no underground streams to provide additional water, it just sits there. Because there is no water flow, there is little oxygen, which is necessary for decaying and composting to occur. Sphagnum moss is one of the few plants that can grow in boggy areas with little oxygen. It serves as nature's cleansing mechanism by secreting acids that inhibit bacterial action. Organisms that die in the bog decay very slowly due to the lack of oxygen; thus, a bog is a good resource for archaeologists to discover what was living in this region thousands of years ago. In addition to its aid to scientific study, sphagnum moss is also useful in gardens for keeping the soil loose and retaining moisture.

Sweet pepperbush

Look around and notice what varieties of plants are growing near the bog. The **swamp azalea**'s sweet-smelling flower, white and vase shaped, blooms in July and August. The **sweet pepperbush**, with its small, fragrant white flowers clustered in short spikes, is another shrub that prefers moist areas.

As you descend on the White Trail toward the beach, observe that the trees become smaller and their branches more stunted and deformed—the result of strong winds that bombard this exposed ridge.

3. Upon reaching the beach turn right.

Look across Vineyard Sound toward the **Elizabeth Islands. Naushon,** the island directly ahead, is the largest of the chain. To the far left lies **Cuttyhunk,** which contains the town of **Gosnold,** the governmental center of the Elizabeth Islands. The other islands are privately owned.

4. Continue past the fenced-in dune-restoration area, one Red Trail marker, and more fences. After approximately a ten-minute walk on the beach, you'll reach the steps marking the entrance to the Brown Trail and the spectacular bluff loop.

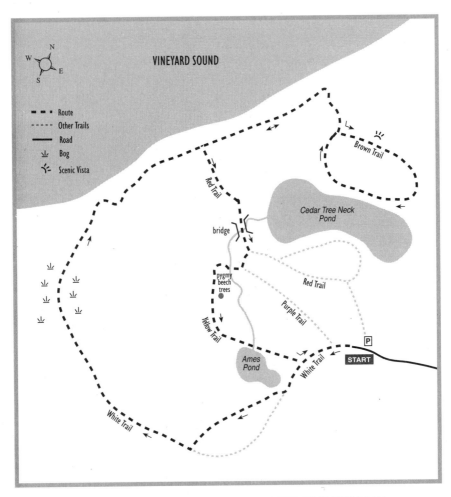

🥾🥾 CEDAR TREE NECK WILDLIFE SANCTUARY

To the right lies Cedar Tree Neck Pond and on the left typical beach vegetation, including ***Rosa rugosa***, bayberry, and pasture rose. During the summer *Rosa rugosa* sports a rose-colored flower, and in the fall the flower has transformed into a large, red rose hip. The **pasture rose** displays a pink flower and five to nine small, egg-shaped leaflets. **Bayberry** is a green shrub with many branches covered with small oblong leaves. If you crush its leaves the distinctive bayberry aroma will fill the air. In late summer and fall the female bayberry develops small, round, hard white berries, which are actually wax-covered nutlets. This waxy coating is used in making candles.

5. Bear left at the fork.

6. On your ascent, turn left into the cleared lookout for a panorama, including the Elizabeth Islands straight ahead and the flickering beam of the Gay Head Lighthouse to the west.

Keep your eye out for **blackberry** bushes that produce large, succulent berries in midsummer. Make sure you avoid the poison ivy.

As the trail veers inland the vegetation changes, and you will find yourself under a cooling canopy formed by the arching branches of sassafras and tupelo trees.

Beach pea and beach grass

7. The trail descends between grapevines and bayberry bushes to the beach. Turn left to walk back beside the fence to the Red Trail.

8. Turn left at the next break in the fence, at the Red Trail marker, back into the sanctuary.

Before you go inland, look down at the **beach grass**. Avoid walking on this plant. Crushing it hinders the grass from performing a most important function: stabilizing dune areas to prevent erosion. Beach grass provides a wonderful lesson in adaptation. It can survive in hot, dry locations because the grass curls to avoid drying out. Feel the grass's rough edges, and you will know why animals are not inclined to nibble on it. **Beach pea** grows amid the beach grass. In the spring it produces purple, pea-shaped flowers which in the summer are replaced by pods.

On your left is another view of Cedar Tree Neck Pond.

9.   Continue straight and cross a plank bridge on the Red Trail as you proceed to the Yellow Trail. Turn right onto the Yellow Trail.

Look up on your left for a grove of Cedar Tree Neck's famous **bonsai (pygmy) beech trees.** These 100-year-old trees normally would have grown to a height of 80 feet, but their exposed location, where they are regularly blasted by the salt-laden wind, prevented them from growing tall. Their wide trunks attest to their age, but their angular horizontal branches have been shaped by fierce, wintry gales.

10.   Bear to the right at the junction with Yellow Trail. Remain on the Yellow Trail as it makes two stream crossings.

Sensitive ferns, sturdy ferns with broad, almost triangular leaves, line the bank at the second stream crossing.

The larger stream empties into Cedar Tree Neck Pond, where the water then travels underground into the ocean.

11.   At the T intersection turn left, following the yellow-blazed Irons Trail to Ames Pond.

This moss-covered rocky trail runs by the pond and provides a wonderful vantage point for viewing the wildlife living there. **Tadpoles** swim along the bottom; tiny **water striders** scoot on top of the water, while **whirligig beetles** run in circles. Turtles, geese, and minuscule frogs called **pinkletinks** often appear. If you are walking in the spring and hear what sounds like a frenzied flock of starlings, you are listening to the high-pitched mating calls of male pinkletinks.

12.   Continue on the Yellow Trail to the intersection with the White Trail. Turn left onto the White Trail to return to the parking lot.

CHAPTER TWENTY-FIVE

Long Point Wildlife Refuge

"No gain without pain" or "seek and ye shall finally find" describes an excursion to Long Point Wildlife Refuge, one of my favorite places on Martha's Vineyard. Why bother traveling over a seemingly endless, narrow, unpaved road? Because at its end lies a magnificent secluded beach flanked by coves and ponds. You can walk for miles along the coast and jump the waves, swim in the calm waters of Long Cove Pond, and explore the refuge's tranquil trails around the pond and cove.

Be aware—their small parking lot fills quickly on a hot summer day. If you don't mind biking on unpaved roads, you never will be refused entry nor will you have to pay the $7 charge for automobiles.

Directions: The summer entrance, open from 10:00 A.M. to 6:00 P.M., June 15 to September 15, is via Waldron's Bottom Road on the south side of the Edgartown–West Tisbury Road, 0.3 mile west of the airport entrance (second dirt road on the left after the airport). Proceed 1.3 miles on Waldron's Bottom Road, turn left, and then make a quick right onto Hughe's Thumb Road. Remain on this road for 1.2 miles to the gatehouse. When the parking lot is full, rangers post a sign at the turnoff from the Edgartown–West Tisbury Road.

The off-season entrance, via Deep Bottom Road, is 0.8 mile farther west on the Edgartown–West Tisbury Road.

Distance: From the parking lot, along the beach, and to and through the trails: 3 miles.

Difficulty: Easy, wide, level trails.

Fees: $7 per car plus $3 for each adult. Children under fifteen and members of the Trustees of Reservations are free.

Restroom: The portable toilet is located east of the parking area.

Background: The Trustees of Reservations, the oldest land trust in the nation, owns and maintains this 633-acre refuge. Three other Trustees properties are described in this book: Menemsha Hills Reservation in Chilmark, and Wasque Reservation and Mytoi on Chappaquiddick.

Long Point Wildlife Refuge is an example of a rare landscape: coastal sandplain created by outwash from the melting glacier. Sand and gravel, picked up by the glacier as it moved southward more than fifteen thousand years ago, were left behind, covering much of the southern side of the island.

At Long Point the sandy soil, strong winds, and salt spray determine which species can survive under such harsh conditions. Some of the rare plants that grow on the sandplain are Nantucket shadbush, bushy rockrose, and sandplain blue-eyed grass. Hundreds and thousands of years ago this prairielike habitat was maintained by frequent fires which prevented overgrown vegetation. Now the Trustees of Reservations have instituted a system of controlled fires, which they hope will encourage the continued existence of the endangered vegetation that has adapted to this sandplain.

Several species of rare birds inhabit this property, including the northern **harrier**, a slender, narrow-winged hawk you may spot soaring over the meadows and ponds. **Common** and **least terns**, white-bodied with black caps, patrol the beach and then dive into the ocean for fish. If you sight a shorebird darting across the sand and then stopping suddenly and taking off, it is probably a variety of **plover**.

THE ROUTE

1. From the summer parking lot, proceed south toward the beach on the path that runs between Long Cove Pond on the right and Big Homer's Pond on the left.

    The numerous small ponds and coves on the southern side of the island originally were created by streams from melting glacial ice. After

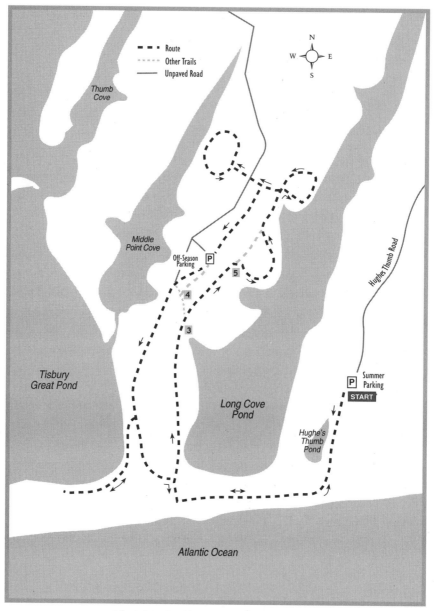

🚶🚶 LONG POINT WILDLIFE REFUGE

the glacier disappeared, the streams dried up, leaving wide openings that filled with a combination of sea water and fresh water from underground springs. These coves and ponds continue to be a mix of fresh and salt water.

Note the vegetation that has adapted to this harsh enviroment. Don't get near the omnipresent **poison ivy** (clusters of three shiny leaves), which thrives in sunny, arid areas. Near the dunes you'll find **beach pea** sprawled on the sand. In the spring this ground-hugging plant produces a purple flower which turns into a pea pod in the summer. In the autumn **seaside goldenrod** decorates the dunes with bright yellow flowers. **Dusty miller** is a bluish gray plant with lacy leaves. Its dusty covering conserves water so that it can survive hot, sunny summers. Be careful not to walk on the **beach grass**, which is essential for maintaining the fragile dunes. The grass preserves moisture in its long blades by curling inward to avoid the sun's drying rays.

2. Upon reaching the beach, turn right and walk past Long Cove Pond until you reach the next beach entrance, identified by an opening in the fenced-in dune area (about a 10-minute walk from the main beach entrance).

3. Turn right onto the path through the sandplain grassland. Long Cove Pond will be on your on your right, and Tisbury Great Pond will be on your left.

The No. 3 marker on the right side of the trail near a marshy section of Long Pond Cove refers to the wildlife that inhabit this section. The narrow paths to the pond were formed by **river otters**, identified by their long, dark-brown bodies and short legs. Look for **snowy egrets**, pure-white birds with long black legs and bright yellow feet, which may be wading in the water.

4. Before you reach the staff residence, turn right at the No. 4 marker.

5. To begin this scenic loop, turn right at the No. 5 marker.

The path meanders through a woodland composed of four varieties of oak trees: white, black, scrub, and post. To identify the **white oak**, look for leaves with five to nine rounded lobes. The **post oak** also has rounded lobes but usually has only five lobes that form the shape of a cross. The **black oak** has lobes with bristly tips, while the **scrub oak** also has leaves with five lobes and bristly tips, but its lobes aren't as deeply cut.

6. Turn right to head for the second loop.

7. Turn right again.

8. Bear right at the fork to enter the second Long Cove Pond Loop. You'll discover a picnic table and benches positioned perfectly to allow its occupants to appreciate the view while they rest or eat. The path enters a pine forest as it continues to follow the shore of Long Cove Pond.

9. After exploring the second loop, turn left.

10. Make a quick right. This path crosses the off-season access road and leads to another loop trail that visits Middle Point Cove.

11. Bear right at the fork to begin the Middle Point Cove Loop.

12. After exploring the loop, take the first right onto a trail that travels through a heavily wooded area filled with bracken ferns, large oaks, and pines.

13. Upon reaching the off-season parking lot, follow the path that runs through the middle of the lot.

14. Bear right at the fork, heading toward the house and Tisbury Great Pond.

15. Cross the road and remain on the path that passes Middle Point Cove and then Tisbury Great Pond.

16. To walk along the pond's shore, follow the trail until it veers close to the pond. Turn right onto a steep boardwalk that leads to the water.

    The water level in the pond depends on whether there is an opening in the barrier beach that separates it from the ocean. Often storms produce a breach, but if there have been no storms, an opening is dug two or three times a year to allow the ocean to flow through to cleanse the pond and maintain its brackish quality.

    Be careful of the shellfish that inhabit the pond. Tisbury Great Pond is seeded for **oysters** whose razor-sharp shells can cut the feet of unwary walkers. Severed pincers of **blue-claw crabs** collect on the sand, but it's the unsevered ones that you should avoid. Low tide draws net-swishing crab-collectors trying to capture the wily crustaceans.

17. After your pond walk, turn right onto the trail.

18. Turn right to the beach.

19. Turn left at the beach to return to the summer entrance.

CHAPTER TWENTY-SIX

Sepiessa Point Reservation

What makes Sepiessa Point Reservation such a great destination on a hot summer day? Its location on Tisbury Great Pond. After hiking or biking on wide, well-maintained paths to scenic Sepiessa Point, you can peel off your clothes and go for a swim at the half-mile-long sandy beach. Bring beach shoes. Because the pond is seeded for oysters, sharp shells are scattered along the beach and in the water.

Directions: On the Edgartown–West Tisbury Road proceed 3 miles west of the entrance to the Martha's Vineyard Airport. Turn left onto New Lane. Follow New Lane for 1.2 miles. Turn right onto Clam Point Road to the reservation.

Distance: 2.5 miles.

Difficulty: Easy.

Food and drink: The closest spot is Alley's General Store and Back Alley Café, 0.4 mile west of the intersection of New Lane and the Edgartown–West Tisbury Road.

Background: The public has fought over access to Tisbury Great Pond since 1674, when Simon Athearn purchased the surrounding land from an Indian named Jude, without getting permission from Thomas Mayhew, the lord proprietor of the island.

Until 1991 there was no public road to the water. Informal access was granted to fishermen, who in exchange presented the landowners with a portion of their catch. As tax assessments increased and parcels of land were subdivided, informal access became more difficult. In an attempt to gain public access to the pond, the town of West Tisbury approached every landowner along the pond. No one was interested in selling until January 1991, when the McAlpin Family let it be known that they wished to sell their 165-acre property. In May 1991 the property was purchased for $1,925,000 by the Martha's Vineyard Land Bank, a conservation organization, which is funded by a 2 percent tax on real estate transfers. One of the main reasons for the Land Bank's purchase of Sepiessa Point was to allow community access to Tisbury Great Pond.

THE ROUTE

1. From the parking lot, proceed straight on the White Trail, which borders Tiah's Cove. Follow the trail as it passes the boat launch site, continues straight for 0.3 mile, and then bears left, crossing the dirt road and entering a pitch pine forest.

    Keep your eyes open for the rare **northern harrier**, a marsh hawk around 2 feet long, which often glides close to the ground searching for prey. The males are pale gray and the females are brown.

2. After walking through a woodland of scrub oak trees with an understory of huckleberry bushes, turn right, remaining on the White Trail.

    The path heads toward Tississa Cove. The clearing near the water allows a full view of the farm on the other side. A fence extends into the water to prevent the owners' goats from drowning.

    Watch for the eaglelike **osprey**, which may be perching on the pole at the southern tip of the farm or plunging feet first into the water in search of fish.

    As the trail approaches Tisbury Great Pond, the trees become smaller and the vegetation sparser due to the wind and salt spray. Growing in this sunny sandplain section are plants that usually are not found on the mainland, such as **sandplain flax**, **Nantucket shadbush**, and **bushy rockrose**. The **caribou moss** growing along the trail is further evidence of the harsh climatic conditions in this area.

3. The path merges with a carriage road. Bear left, heading toward the pond. A side trail, blazed blue, leads to the parking area for the beach and the second boat launch site.

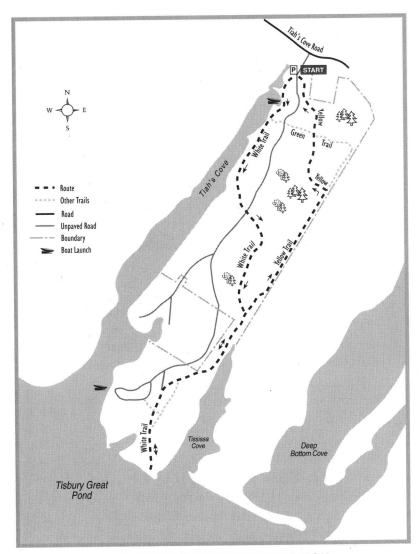

🚶🚶 SEPIESSA POINT PRESERVATION

4. The trail ends at the shore.

Oyster shells scattered on the sand are the result of oyster seeding in the pond. Since oysters require salt water to breed, twice a year a breach is created in the barrier beach to allow the ocean to flow through to the pond.

If you visit Sepiessa Point soon after the breach is dug, you'll find a much larger beach, as the water level in the pond recedes significantly.

Tississa Cove.

Blue-claw crabs also inhabit Tisbury Great Pond. During low tide you may spot waders armed with nets attempting to scoop up the fast-moving crabs.

As you walk along the beach, you may be able to spot a few of the ten coves and ponds that extend out from Tisbury Great Pond like fingers on a hand, with Black Point Pond forming the thumb. Sepiessa Point lies between Tiah's Cove and Tississa Cove. Beyond Tississa Cove, on the left, are Deep Bottom and Thumb Coves, which border **Long Point Reservation**, the Trustees of Reservations property that is explored in chapter 25. These coves and pond are among a series that span the southern side of Martha's Vineyard and are separated from the Atlantic Ocean by thin strips of barrier beach.

5. To return, retrace your route on the White Trail.

6. At the junction with the Yellow Trail, bear right onto the Yellow Trail.

7. At the junction with the Green Trail, turn left, remaining on the Yellow Trail to the dirt road.

8. Cross the intersection with the Green Trail, and stay on the Yellow until you return to the parking lot.

CHAPTER TWENTY-SEVEN

Middle Road Sanctuary

My favorite time of year to hike around tranquil Middle Road Sanctuary is midsummer, when blueberries and huckleberries are at their peak. Oak trees provide shade as I nibble the succulent berries and climb the trail that overlooks the south coast and Chilmark Pond. I compete for the berries with a wide variety of birds that inhabit the sanctuary, including great-crested flycatchers, downy and hairy woodpeckers, red-tailed hawks, white-breasted nuthatches, rufous-sided towhees, Carolina wrens, and chickadees.

Directions: From the intersection of Middle Road and Music Street in West Tisbury, proceed 2.1 miles on Middle Road. The parking lot and sanctuary are on the left (soon after passing Tea Lane on the right).

Distance: 2.7 miles.

Difficulty: Moderate; a long gradual climb.

Food and drink: The closest shops are on South Road, just west of Chilmark Center (2.3 miles). The Chilmark Store is known for its pizza and frozen coffee drinks, and Chilmark Chocolates creates the best candy on the island.

Background: We must credit the last glacier for the sanctuary's distinctive terrain. About fifteen thousand years ago, as the glacier inched its way southward, it finally stopped and began to melt at Middle Road Sanctuary (and the surrounding latitude). This last stopping point, called a terminal moraine, contains the characteristic steep ridges and valleys that result from glacial melting. Along with blueberry bushes, the sanctuary also boasts glacial erratics, boulders pulled from the bedrock and then left behind when the glacier melted.

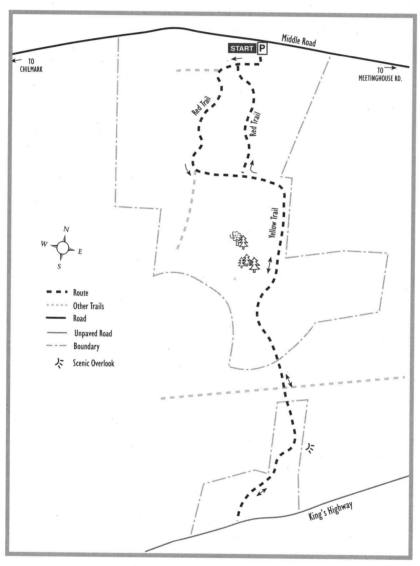

🚶🚶 MIDDLE ROAD SANCTUARY

.The Sheriff's Meadow Foundation owns and manages this 110-acre sanctuary. Over the last thirty-five years, the Sheriff's Meadow Foundation has acquired and received more than two thousand acres of land on Martha's Vineyard. Some of these properties are protected land and not open to the public. Others, like Middle Road Sanctuary, provide visitors with the opportunity for a relaxing hike through varied island terrain. The name "sanctuary" describes how the foundation wants its property to be used: communing with nature is fine, but neither biking, picnicking, nor camping is allowed. However, there are no rules prohibiting berry-picking!

THE ROUTE

1. From the parking lot, head onto the trail.
2. At the fork bear right onto the Red Trail.

   This trail loops around through typical Vineyard woodland: black, white, and scarlet oak trees above, with an underlayer of huckleberry, blueberry, and bayberry bushes. The huckleberry and blueberry bushes have similar small, green, oval leaves. Their berries differ, although both are equally tasty. The **huckleberry** is black and contains a tiny seed that crunches when chewed. The **blueberry** is blue with a powdery surface. The **bayberry** has a larger oval leaf which when crushed emits the familiar, fragrant bayberry scent. Its small, round, hard white berries, attached to the base of the stem, fortify birds during winter.

Wild grape

Bayberry

3. Bear left onto what used to be an old carriage road, remaining on the Red Trail.

4. Leave the old road and turn left, continuing on the Red Trail.

5. Proceed straight onto the mile-long Yellow Trail.

   This route ascends to the peak and winds through more diverse vegetation, courtesy of the clay soil that holds water closer to the surface than on the sandier Red Trail. **Bracken ferns** and **cinnamon ferns** line the path and **wild grapes** climb over oak tree branches and viburnum bushes. For a short distance the trail parallels a stone wall that formerly served as a boundary line between the sheep farms that occupied this land.

6. The path meets an unpaved road. Cross the road and look directly ahead for the Yellow Trail marker. Continue on the path, passing a house on the right.

   The gnarled branches of the low scrub oak trees result from winds that batter this peak. Soon you will come to a short path on the left where a glacial erratic sits under a **black oak** tree. Behind the erratic lies a vista of Chilmark Pond and the Atlantic Ocean. The trail meanders through a heavily wooded section until it ends at an ancient dirt road named the King's Highway. If you turn left and follow it for almost a 0.5 mile, you'll reach another old unpaved way, named Meetinghouse Road. Another left turn and an additional 0.7 mile will return you to Middle Road. To return to the sanctuary, make another left turn onto Middle Road.

7. If you are returning via the same route, follow the Yellow Trail until it merges with the Red Trail.

8. Turn right onto the Red Trail to hike the remaining 0.3 mile to the entrance.

   Again, you'll hike through an oak woodland with an undergrowth of huckleberry bushes. Another large glacial erratic appears on the left.

CHAPTER TWENTY-EIGHT

Fulling Mill Brook Preserve

Sound effects accompany you on this hike to one of my favorite picnic spots on Martha's Vineyard. The route follows a gurgling brook that meanders through a forest bursting with bird songs. You can munch your lunch on the boulder-lined bank of Fulling Mill Brook. The postlunch return rambles across meadows and through woodland.

Directions: Proceed southwest on Middle Road for 3.2 miles. Turn left onto Henry Hough Lane (the street after Fulling Mill Brook Road) and left again into the parking lot that holds a bike rack. The South Road entrance, 1 mile west of Meetinghouse Road, also has a bike rack and parking for several cars.

Distance: 2.25 miles.

Difficulty: Moderate. The first half of the walk on the Green Trail is hilly; the return is on level ground.

Food and drink: The closest stores are in Chilmark Center, 1 mile west on Middle Road.

Background: This forty-six-acre property is owned jointly by the town of Chilmark and the Martha's Vineyard Land Bank Commission, an island-funded conservation organization. The name of the property was derived from the fulling mill that operated here from 1694 to 1770. "Fulling" is a term that refers to an early method of removing oil and grease from wool by using hydrated aluminum and magnesium silicate. At the fulling mill workers first cleaned, shrunk, and thickened the wool. Then, running water from the brook propelled hammers that pounded large pieces of wool until it became smooth enough to use for making clothes.

THE ROUTE

1. From the parking lot, walk behind the trail board onto the Yellow Trail, where you will navigate your first brook crossing (easy—up the stairs and over the walkway). The trail ascends before it meets a dirt road.

    On the left side, just before the road, a giant boulder serves as a backdrop for a large **American beech** tree. Note its smooth, mottled gray bark and toothed, elliptical leaves. Beech trees favor moist areas, so you will find them along the Green Trail.

2. Cross the dirt road and begin the Green Trail.

    Several varieties of small lacy ferns: **marsh, evergreen wood,** and **Massachusetts** grow near the banks of the river. Larger, moisture-loving ferns—royal and cinnamon—grow along the trail. You can distinguish between the two by looking closely at the leaflets: the **royal fern** has distinct oval-shaped leaflets, while the leaflets on the **cinnamon fern** are etched out of its stem.

Royal fern

Cinnamon fern

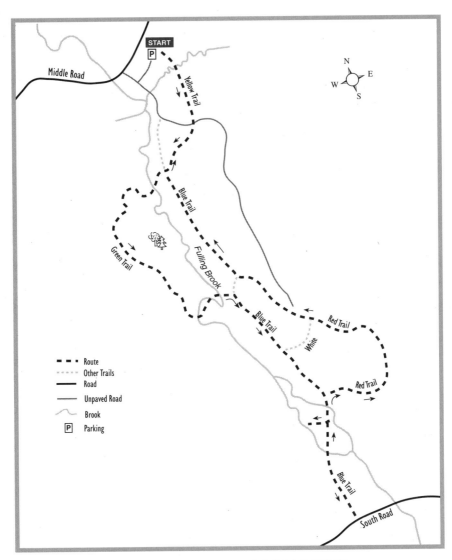

🚶🚶 FULLING MILL BROOK PRESERVE

The trail passes by a mossy glacial erratic, a boulder picked up by the glacier and then deposited fifteen thousand years ago when the glacier began to melt. The path descends and crosses another trail. A long, narrow bridge signals another brook crossing. A steep incline climbs to the crest of a hill covered with grapevines and prickly greenbrier. A quick descent leads to a tiny wood-plank bridge. The trail cuts across two old stone walls before it ascends to the top of another hill. Look to your left for a clearing with a seascape of the south side of the island.

A bench rests above steep stairs that lead to a long, narrow board-walk. Proceed across a wetland and then the Fulling Mill Brook.

White oak

Sassafras, black cherry, and American beech trees grow near the riverbed. It's easy to spot the **sassafras** tree. Look for leaves that have three distinct shapes—one with one lobe, another with two lobes that look like a mitten, and the third with three lobes.

Tupelo trees also prefer a moist habitat. This species is easiest to spot in autumn, when its small, oval-shaped leaves turn bright orange and red. The tupelo tree also is called **black gum** and, on Martha's Vineyard, **beetlebung**.

On the left, just before the end of the boardwalk, a **red (swamp) maple** tree bends across the riverbank. Its trunk has split in half, with one half growing horizontally, parallel to the boardwalk.

3.   Turn right onto the Blue Trail, the old carriage lane that connects Middle and South Roads.

In early summer round, white blooms on the **shadbush** decorate the sides of the trail.

4.   The path enters a meadow and then returns to a woodland. After re-entering the woods, look to your right for an unmarked path that leads to the boulder-lined banks of the Fulling Mill Brook.

Large flat rocks line both sides of the brook and make perfect picnic tables. A tiny waterfall adds just the right sound effect. Although the water looks inviting, do not drink it. Please carry out your trash.

5. Return to the Blue Trail. Turn right to follow the carriage road to imposing stone columns that once flanked what was the main entrance to the mill.

   The Tilton family, descendants of the owners of the fulling mill, established a gristmill here in 1850. They used rushing water from the brook to rotate heavy stones that ground the grain.

6. Retrace your route on the Blue Trail.

7. As soon as you leave the woods and enter the meadow, look to your right for the beginning of the Red Trail. Turn right.

   The dry woodlands and meadows along the Red Trail contrast with the lush wetlands of the Green Trail. Here the vegetation consists mainly of **black and white oaks**, often with an understory of **bayberry** bushes, distinguished by their waxy, green leaves. An old **maple** tree with mottled bark and wide branches sits on the left side, 0.2 mile from the beginning of the Red Trail. It provides shelter for anyone in need of an excuse to stop and rest.

8. Continue straight as the trail passes the intersection with the White Trail, a spur that connects the Red and Blue Trails.

9. The Red Trail cuts through a stone wall right before its intersection with the Blue Trail. Turn right onto the Blue Trail.

10. Turn right onto the Yellow Trail and retrace your original route.

CHAPTER TWENTY-NINE

Peaked Hill Reservation

Mountain climbing on Martha's Vineyard? Well, not quite. Climbing to a 311-foot summit is about as close as you are going to get. But the view from the top does offer a mountain-size view of the south shore, Aquinnah (Gay Head), and Elizabeth Islands. If you scale the peak in August, your reward will be bountiful blueberries and blackberries.

Directions: From the intersection of Middle and Tabor House Roads, go 0.5 mile. Turn left (opposite the Chilmark landfill) onto a dirt road. (From the intersection of North and Tabor House Roads, go 0.5 mile and turn right.) Follow the dirt road for 0.7 mile and turn right at the fork to reach the entrance.

Distance: 1.5 miles

Difficulty: Moderate; two steep hills

Background: Much of the reservation is bordered by stone walls built with rocks left behind when the last glacier melted. Farmers cleared their rocky land and piled rocks to form walls to define boundaries and restrain livestock. On Peaked Hill the stone walls contained sheep that grazed there.

At the beginning of World War II the military took advantage of this elevated eastern location and installed a radar station on top of what is now called Radar Hill. During the Korean War the government added a communications facility.

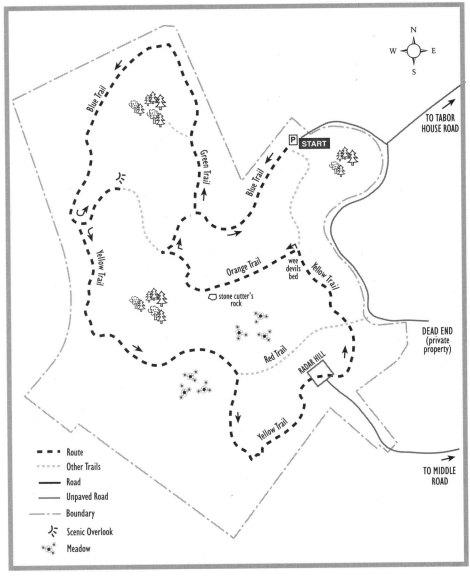

PEAKED HILL RESERVATION

The property became conservation land in 1970, when the government auctioned it off to residents, who then donated the land to the Vineyard Open Land Foundation (VOLF). Perhaps the reason why the government sold the land, and no developer jumped at the chance to take advantage of the fabulous view, was the same—no water. Finding a location to drill a well proved impossible, so all water had to be hauled up to the top of Radar Hill. The property is now managed by the Land Bank, which purchased it from VOLF in 1992.

THE ROUTE

1. From the parking lot, head off to the right onto the Blue Trail.

   During the summer the trail is lined with tall yellow flowers called **stiff goldenrod**. White, flat-topped **Queen Anne's lace** and **black-eyed Susan**, with bright yellow petals and a black center, decorate the woodland. Each of the bright blue blooms on the **chicory** plant lasts only a day.

Hay-scented fern

2. Bear right at the fork onto the Green Trail.

3. Take the next right onto the Blue Trail.

   Blackberries, blueberries, and huckleberries border the path. After passing a stone wall on your right, you'll come to a thicket of ferns. The **hay-scented fern** has long, pale green fronds that are shaped like a Christmas tree, wide at the bottom and tapering to its tip. Its name is derived from the odor released when its fronds are crushed. The **bracken fern** is easily identified because its leaves grow in clusters of three. The dainty **lady fern** grows in circular clusters.

   The trail then runs through woodland and meadow.

4. After ascending, continue straight on the Blue Trail. A spur on the left reveals a view of the

Bracken fern

south shore and the tiny, government-owned island named Noman's Land.

5. Retrace your steps to the intersection with the Yellow Trail. Turn left.

    Follow the Yellow Trail on the way to Radar Hill lookout. The trail winds among blueberry and huckleberry bushes to a meadow on the right filled with blackberry bushes, protected from hungry hikers by their prickly stems. The **sweet pepperbush** indicates that the terrain has become lower and moister. Its name refers to the sweet smell emitted by small white flowers growing from the tips of its branches.

    The trail meanders through a meadow dotted with yellow wildflowers: **hawkweed** with small narrow petals and the small, bushy **wild indigo**, which produces tiny pealike flowers. Glacial erratics, boulders left by the glacier when it melted, are scattered around the meadow.

    You may notice a wire fence surrounding an apple tree sapling. It was placed there by the Land Bank to prevent deer from destroying the tree.

6. Bear right onto the Yellow Trail as it passes the Red Trail on the left and ascends through an oak woodland to Radar Hill for another panorama.

    Looking west, Menemsha Pond is the closest body of water. Squibnocket Pond lies just beyond. To the northwest stands Gay Head Lighthouse and its cliffs.

7. Cross the parking lot and pick up the Yellow Trail on the left. The path crosses a carriage road (Red Trail). If hungry, watch for blueberry bushes on both sides of the trail.

8. Turn left onto the Orange Trail. If tired, head to the left side of the trail intersection to rest on a low, flat erratic called "wee devil's bed."

9. Turn left onto a short side trail to view Stonecutter's Rock. You'll find three long vertical chunks that have been cut from a huge boulder. If you look closely at the boulder, you'll spot several drill holes.

10. Return to the Orange Trail and turn left.

11. Take the next right onto the Blue Trail.

12. Turn right onto the carriage road (Blue Trail) to return to the trailhead.

CHAPTER THIRTY

Great Rock Bight Preserve

Finally—a spot on the north shore where you can hike and swim. Great Rock Bight Preserve, a recent acquisition by the Martha's Vineyard Land Bank, was worth the wait. It offers a handicapped-accessible, shady, wide, level walking trail with benches at which you can stop to admire vistas of Vineyard Sound and the Elizabeth Islands. A steeper trail leads to a sheltered bay where the "great rock" guards a sandy beach that runs for 1,300 feet beside the calm waters of Vineyard Sound.

Get there early, as there are only eighteen spaces in the parking lot. A property attendant oversees the parking area and another is stationed on the beach.

Directions: The preserve is located on the right side of North Road, 3.7 miles west of the intersection of State, North, and South roads in West Tisbury, 1.2 miles west of Tea Lane, and just past the Chilmark fire station. To reach the parking lot and trailhead, proceed 0.5 mile down the entrance road.

Distance: 1.5 miles, including beach walk; 0.4 mile handicapped-accesssible loop; 0.5 mile direct route to beach

Difficulty: Generally easy walking, but the descent to the beach is steep

Restrooms: Located on the left of the trailhead.

Food and drink: The Galley, the Deli, and Menemsha Market are located in Menemsha, 2 miles southwest of the preserve.

Background: One of the earliest owners of the land was Elisha Amos, a Wampanoag who died in 1763. He married his slave, Rebecca, who inherited the property and continued to farm here until she died in 1801.

This land not only was used for farming but also provided materials for a brick factory. In the mid-1800s workers dug clay, formed bricks, and baked 600,000 of them a year. Trees were chopped down to fuel the ovens that baked the bricks. After twenty years of operation, all the trees on the land

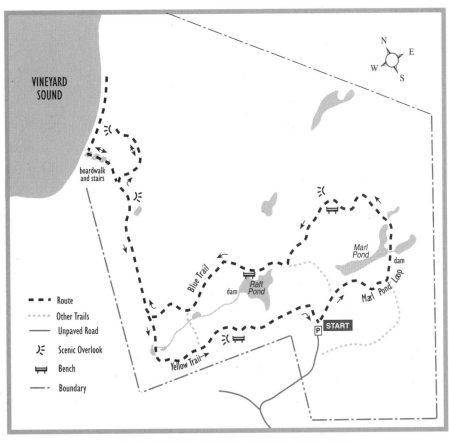

🚶🚶 GREAT ROCK BIGHT PRESERVE

had been felled. With no fuel, the factory closed and the property reverted to farmland.

THE ROUTE

1. From the trailhead, walk down the path and turn right to begin the Marl Pond Loop. A boardwalk crosses over Marl Pond, a man-made pond dug by the former owners to provide water for their livestock. This shady, damp area attracts several varieties of ferns. The aptly named **marsh fern**, growing to the left of the first boardwalk, thrives in damp soil. Look for a delicate fern whose leaves grow opposite each other on a smooth, pale-green stalk. **Sassafras** trees also prefer moist areas and are common to these woods. Its unusual three-lobed leaves make them easy to spot. Under the trees grows **Indian cucumber-root**. Early Native American inhabitants were fond of the root, which smells and tastes a lot like cucumber. To identify Indian cucumber-root, look for a plant with two layers—one whorl of oblong leaves above and another below. Its small yellow-green flowers emerge from the top layer in the spring. At the same time of year the **starflower** produces two small, white, starlike flowers that pop out from the center of five or six shiny, dark-green leaves.

Indian cucumber-root

    Early settlers also dined on the **common evening primrose**, whose roots resemble carrots and leaves taste similar to lettuce. Now the plant is valued for the curative qualities of its oil, which is touted as reducing inflammation, easing the itching of eczema, and speeding the healing of wounds. Its name refers to the time of day when its showy yellow flowers open. The blooms of this biennial can be as high as 5 feet but appear only in its second year.

    In late summer many of the hundred varieties of asters dot the woodland. The **small white aster** is typical of asters that seek these moist open places.

2. At the junction with the Blue Trail, turn right to head down toward the beach.

    Raft Pond, also man-made, appears on the left. You may spot snapping and painted turtles resting on the banks. The bench offers a terrific view across Vineyard Sound to the Elizabeth Islands.

3. Before you turn right to begin your descent to the beach, look on your left at the plaque attached to a large boulder. It designates the African-American Heritage Trail and is also a tribute to Elisha Amos's wife Rebecca, an African slave who died a free woman.

4. Bear right at the fork for a quick stop at the lookout for a spectacular panorama that encompasses Aquinnah on the left and the Elizabeth Islands ahead (the largest, Naushon is straight on).

5. Return to the trail and turn right to head down to the beach.

    Here you'll find ferns that grow in dry areas, such as the delicate, medium-sized, yellowish green **New York fern**. To distinguish the New York fern from other varieties, look for three or more leaves rising from its root stock.

    Sun-loving plants that grow in this arid environment include **beach pea, beach rose**, and **seaside goldenrod**. In the spring beach pea decorates the sand with dainty purple flowers that turn to pods in the summer. The bright yellow flowers of seaside goldenrod contrast with the beach rose's pink blooms.

6. Walk along the beach.

7. To return, head back on the same trail.

8. At the African-American Heritage Trail Boulder intersection, bear right onto the Yellow Trail to return on the other half of the loop.

    This open area is filled with grapevines and blackberry bushes. After walking about five minutes, you'll come to a cluster of **tupelos**, also called black gum and, here on the island, beetlebung trees. In the autumn, their small, shiny, oval green leaves turn bright red.

9. Turn right to return to the parking lot.

CHAPTER THIRTY-ONE

Menemsha Hills Reservation

Head for Menemsha Hills for a good workout on a variety of terrain. The reservation boasts four different ecosystems within its 211 acres, including nearly 1 mile of rocky coast. The high point of a tour around Menemsha Hills is hiking to the top of Prospect Hill for a panorama of both the north and south coasts.

Directions: The reservation is located on the north side of North Road, one mile east of Menemsha Village and 4.7 miles west of the intersection with State Road in North Tisbury.

Distance: 3 miles

Difficulty: Moderate. Wear shoes suitable for hiking up hills and descending on slippery gravel. Take along a water bottle. Many of the trails are exposed, so you can dehydrate quickly on a sunny day.

Restrooms: A portable toilet hides behind a lattice cedar fence at the rear of the parking lot.

Food and drink: At the end of North Road in Menemsha Village, the Galley specializes in lobster rolls and soft-serve ice cream. Next door, the Menemsha Store sells a variety of food and drink.

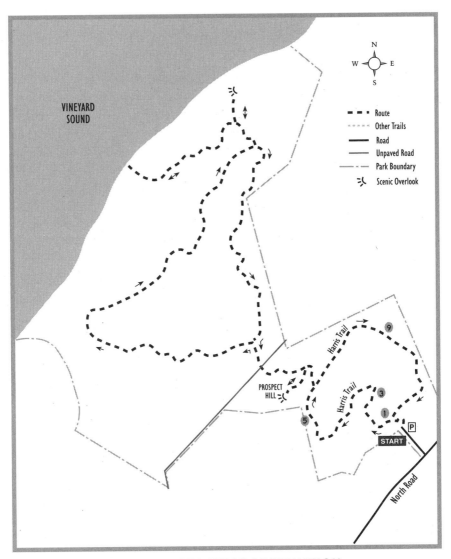

VINEYARD SOUND

N
W   E
S

Route
Other Trails
Road
Unpaved Road
Park Boundary
Scenic Overlook

Harris Trail

Harris Trail

PROSPECT HILL

START

P

North Road

🚶🚶 MENEMSHA HILLS RESERVATION

Background: Prospect Hill marks the farthest reach of the last glacier, which moved southward from the Hudson Bay area twenty thousand to thirty thousand years ago. During its slow journey, the glacier collected much of the surface landscape; when it melted, it deposited its accumulation of stones, boulders, clay, and other debris. This glacial deposit, called a terminal moraine, formed Prospect Hill. Further evidence of glacial melt is seen along the rocky beach.

Menemsha Hills is the most recently developed of the five Trustees of Reservations properties described in this book. The Trustees, the oldest land trust in the nation, is a nonprofit Massachusetts organization dedicated to preserving areas of exceptional scenic, historic, and ecological value. The Trustees have owned this beachfront property since 1966, but it was difficult to reach. The Trustees acquired the land that abuts North Road in 1987, making it possible for visitors to have easier access to the reservation.

THE ROUTE

The trail intersections are color coded: yellow-blazed trails lead to the beach and red blazes lead to the parking lot.

1. From the parking lot and bike rack, head north toward the trail map board. Pick up the trail behind the board.

2. Bear left at the fork to begin the Harris Trail, marked with red blazes.

   The No. 1 marker on the right side of the trail refers to the **beech** trees growing in this section. Look for trees with smooth gray bark and small leaves with large veins and serrated edges.

Beech

   In July the trail is brightened by large white flowers that grow on tall **viburnum** bushes. Later in the month you can feast on blueberries growing next to the trail.

   No. 3 on the right marks a glacial erratic, a large boulder pulled from bedrock by the ice sheet as it inched its way southward. When the ice melted, the boulder remained.

   No. 4 points out a stone wall, a remnant from the nineteenth century, when the land was used for farming and the walls were built to contain sheep.

3. At the fork, bear left and begin your hike to the peak.

4.   Turn left to proceed 0.1 mile.

The pile of rocks on the boulder is a competitive effort to add a few feet to **Prospect Hill**, making it 313 feet so that it will have the distinction of being 2 feet higher than Peaked Hill, now the second highest point on the Vineyard.

From the peak, looking north at the water you can see Vineyard Sound, the Elizabeth Islands, Buzzards Bay, and the Massachusetts coast. If the day is clear, you may spot four Elizabeth Islands: Cuttyhunk, Nashawena, Pasque, and Naushon. A western view includes Menemsha and its harbor, Lobsterville Beach, and Aquinnah (Gay Head). To the southwest you'll see Menemsha Pond, Squibnocket Pond, and the Atlantic Ocean.

5.   Retrace your steps as you return to the fork.

6.   Turn left onto the trail that leads to the Great Sand Cliffs.

The path crosses a dirt road, travels through a brushy section and a scrub oak woodland, and then weaves through an area with topography quite different from Prospect Hill. In August and September poisonous red mushrooms, *Emetic russula*, dot the woods.

Boulder-strewn north shore beach in the Menemsha Hills Reservation.

Watch your footing on your descent, while admiring views of Vineyard Sound, Aquinnah, and Lobsterville Beach.

After the trail becomes level, it heads into a forest of spindly stemmed **horse chestnut** trees. Look for pinwheel-shaped leaves with five, six, or seven leaflets. In late spring, the horse chestnut tree displays white, bell-shaped flowers. In late summer it produces a brown spiny capsule which contains two poisonous chestnutlike seeds. Horse chestnut trees prefer moist soil and are often found in or near wetlands. Grapevines flank the path before it crosses a small wooden bridge that traverses the lowest point of the reservation.

7. After hiking about a mile on this lower trail, turn left, following the yellow blazes toward the beach.

    Yarrow

    A short side trail on the right leads to a lookout for a panorama including a great view of the Elizabeth Islands. Woods Hole and Falmouth are part of the large land mass to the far right. On a clear day the Aquinnah Lighthouse appears on the left.

    A near view on the right reveals a chimney poking through the trees and a boulder perched in the water. The chimney belonged to a brickyard that occupied the land a century ago, and the boulder is the namesake "great rock" of Great Rock Bight Preserve, described in chapter 30.

8. Return to the path and continue down the steep slope to the beach.

    Bearberry, the ground-hugging plant with tiny, shiny green leaves, covers the ledge on both sides of the trail. On your descent into a sunny valley with a great vista of Vineyard Sound and the Elizabeth Islands, you'll see a variety of colorful wildflowers decorating the plain. The white flower with lacy leaves is called **yarrow. *Rosa rugosa's*** pink blossoms cover the hillside. Stay away from the poison ivy encroaching on the trail.

Jump down onto the boulder-strewn beach. The glacier deposited rocks and boulders on the northern side of Martha's Vineyard. Because the southern side is made up of outwash—sand and gravel that flowed from the melting glacier—the beaches there are sandier and usually rock free.

The steep cliff rising from the beach was created by fierce winter winds that hammer the coastline and blow beach sand up the cliff at a 45° angle.

9. To return, retrace your steps on the same trail.

10. Pass the left turn to the overlook and continue straight, following the red blazes back to the entrance.

This half of the lower loop is shorter and less steep. It is filled with unusual oak trees, which have several trunks and long branches that extend out, rather than up. These multiple trunks may be due to sheep having grazed on the oaks' new shoots, or farmers repeatedly cutting down the trees. The determined saplings then sent out new shoots and grew additional stems. Their branches grew horizontally for two reasons: an adaptation for protection from continual wind blasts and to ensure that each branch received as much sun as possible.

11. At the fork, following the red blazes, bear left to the Harris Trail Loop. Recross the road, cut through a stone wall, and pass the path to the top of Prospect Hill.

The trail descends through a moist, wooded section covered with ferns. Among the varieties is the **northern lady fern**. Look for a lacy fern that grows in a circular cluster. Do not get too attached to the prickly greenbrier vines and blackberry bushes.

The No. 9 marker points out **tupelo** trees, also known as black gum. Here on the Vineyard, they're referred to as beetlebung trees because their dense wood was used to construct "bungs," or plugs for barrels that held whale oil, and "beetles," the hammers used to pound in the bungs. The branches of the tupelo tree extend horizontally and display small green leaves that turn bright red in the fall.

12. Turn left to return to the parking lot.

CHAPTER THIRTY-TWO

Aquinnah (Gay Head) Cliffs
Aquinnah Beach

Choose a clear, sunny day to fully appreciate the panorama from the top of Aquinnah Cliffs and for strolling along the beach. From the sand, your eyes will be drawn first to the majestic cliffs, rising steeply to flaunt their colorful striations, and then to the beach-goers, in bathing and birthday suits, prancing in and out of the water and often wallowing—illegally—in the clay pits.

Directions: Travel west on South Road to your first stop in the town of Aquinnah. Continue 1 mile to reach the beach parking lot. The beach is located south of and below the parking lot. The viewing area at the top of the cliffs sits north of and above the lot.

Distance: A short hike to the top of the cliffs; a ten-minute walk down to the beach, and unlimited beach walking

Difficulty: Easy; short climbs from the beach to the parking lot and to the top of the cliffs; level beach walking

Food and drink: Several fast-food shops line the cliffs. For sit-down dining and great views, head for the restaurant Aquinnah on top of the cliffs .

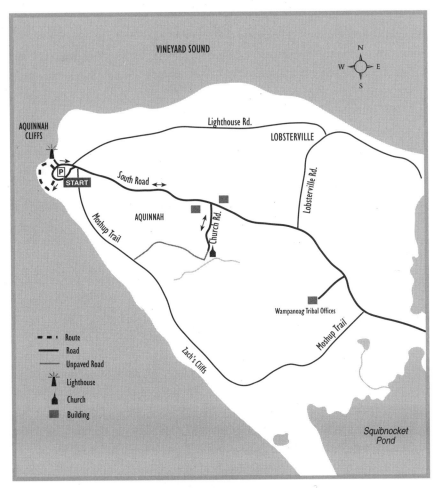

🚶🚶 AQUINNAH

Restrooms: There is a fee to use the bathrooms adjacent to the parking lot. Free portable toilets sit next to the boardwalk at the beach entrance.

Fees: The Aquinnah Lighthouse charges adults $2 to enter. Children under twelve are free.

Background: The Aquinnah Cliffs were created during the Ice Age. Glacial movement and melting forced the upheaval of deposits formed millions of years ago. These deposits flattened into layers, or striations, containing sediments formed during a specific time period and representing a specific geological period. Some layers are composed of fossils, shells, or ancient vegetation, while others consist only of sand or gravel. This upheaval, combined with thousands of years of erosion, has enabled geologists to detect in the cliffs various shadings and textures and the remnants of life, as it was, during the past hundred million years.

The restaurant Aquinnah, at the top of the shop-lined cliff, is named for the tribe of Wampanoag Indians that settled in Aquinnah. Although Aquinnah is now the least populated Vineyard town, its location at the tip of the island was preferred by its Native American settlers because it allowed them to easily travel north, south, or west. The Aquinnahs were proficient seamen and thus were in demand for guiding whaling ships through these treacherous waters. When the European colonists arrived on the island, the Aquinnahs shared their knowledge of the sea and also taught the colonists how to cook fish and shellfish on the sand—the predecessor of our seaside clambakes.

THE ROUTE

1. Aquinnah Center is composed of a volunteer firehouse, the town hall containing the police station, and, across the street, a library housed in a former one-room schoolhouse.

    The schoolhouse was built in 1827 and enlarged in 1857. Boys and girls entered the building separately through its two doors.

2. Turn left onto Old South Road, to the left of the library. This street continues to Moshups Trail and was formerly the main road in the town.

    Bear left onto a gravel road to see the oldest **Native American Baptist church** in continuous existence in North America. It began in 1693 as the first Christian gathering of Wampanoags.

3. Proceed 1 mile to the beach and cliffs parking area.

4. From the parking lot, head up the steps to the viewing area at the top of the Aquinnah Cliffs.

    Look directly north for a splendid seascape of the Elizabeth Islands. The island farthest to the left is Cuttyhunk, the governmental center of the chain. Cuttyhunk appears larger than it actually is because the angle of vision conceals the water that separates it from Nashawena, the island to its right. The next island is Pasque, followed by Naushon. The land mass beyond the islands is Cape Cod.

The **Aquinnah Lighthouse**, perched on the cliffs directly to the right of the viewing area, warns ships away from the wide reef that extends a mile out into the water. The original lighthouse was built in 1799. Its exterior and workings were made of wood that expanded in damp weather, forcing the lighthouse keeper and his wife to turn the light by hand. The current lighthouse, now made of brick, replaced the wooden one in 1844. Twelve years later it was outfitted with a Fresnel lens that captivated the World's Fair in Paris, where it won a gold medal. It now rests in the Vineyard Museum in Edgartown. The Aquinnah Light is maintained by the Martha's Vineyard Historical Society and is open to the public one hour before and one hour after sunset.

Glimpse below the lighthouse for an excellent view of the striated cliffs that end in a secluded beach. The cliffs' sediment layers, colored with shades of red, green, brown, and gray, recount millions of years of

The lighthouse above the Aquinnah Cliffs.

geological deposits. Each color represents a separate period consisting of thousands, and often millions, of years.

5. To head down to the beach, return to the parking lot.

6. Find the boardwalk trail at the southern side of the parking lot and follow it to the beach.

7. Now at the beach, turn right.

    This hike is as good as beach walking gets. Because the beach follows the cliffs around the western tip of the island, the vista out onto the ocean continually changes. The cliffs, the only constant, loom over the beach, providing a multicolored presence at your side. Their colors vary depending on your location, the weather, and the time of day, from midday tones of amber and slate to warm reds and oranges at sunset. As the ocean encroaches, these exposed layers of sedimentary deposit are being worn away.

    The beach's southern side exhibits an assortment of rocks scattered by the frequent storms that have battered this shore. The beach tends to be sandier on this side, and families settle here to swim and picnic. Once you round the bend and head up the rockier northern coast, you'll notice changes in both the beach and its occcupants. Because this section is more remote, it attracts couples who wish to sun and swim unencumbered by bathing suits. Some wallow in the clay at the foot of the cliffs and emerge coated with the dirt. However, environmentalists are rightfully concerned about the clay bathing, since it accelerates the already rapid erosion of the cliffs. Now the clay baths are illegal, and anyone caught partaking of that pleasure pays a hefty fine.

    Once you reach the tip, look directly ahead out onto the ocean for the small, uninhabited **Noman's Land Island**. The island was not always deserted. In the nineteenth century Vineyard fishermen spent at least six months a year there, lobstering in the summer and fishing for cod in the spring and fall. Now Noman's Land Island is living up to its name and is used only by the United States Navy for bombing practice.

    If you continue to walk the beach, you will reach the secluded section you observed from the top of the cliffs.

8. Whenever you finish your tour, do an "about-face" and return.

CHAPTER THIRTY-THREE

Katama Bay

If you are looking for visual variety, head for Katama Bay, where grand Edgartown mansions overlook the water and luxurious yachts rest in the harbor. Across the bay from Edgartown you'll find more-relaxed paddling along Chappaquiddick's bucolic coast and on tranquil Caleb's Pond. Boat traffic increases as you paddle north toward Edgartown Harbor. You can stop and swim anywhere along the 2-mile-long barrier beach that connects Edgartown to Chappaquiddick—and refutes the notion that Chappaquiddick is an island.

This shallow bay draws clam-diggers and scallopers but should be avoided by boaters during low tide, so do check the local newspaper for the tide table before you visit.

Directions: The boat launch is located in Edgartown on Edgartown Bay Road. Follow Katama Road south for 1.6 miles. Turn left onto Edgartown Bay Road. Proceed 0.8 mile, passing Katama Point Preserve, to the boat-launch parking area on the left.

Size: 2.2 miles wide and 3 miles long; allow three to four hours to circle the bay.

Difficulty: Moderate. The southern side of the bay is fairly exposed, so paddling on a windy day can be challenging. Southwest winds generally pick up in mid-afternoon. If you head into Edgartown Harbor, you may encounter boat traffic.

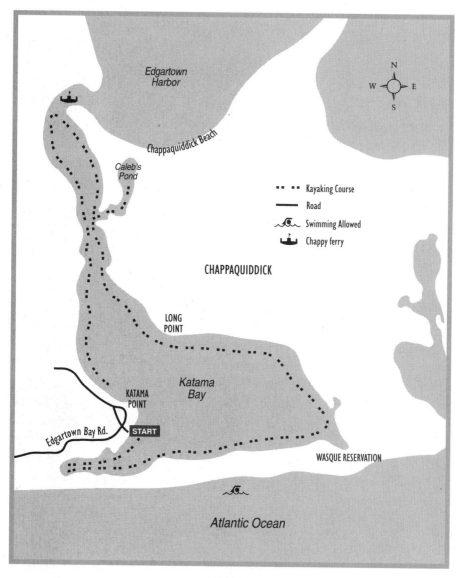

Edgartown
Harbor

Chappaquiddick Beach

Caleb's
Pond

- - - - Kayaking Course
——— Road
Swimming Allowed
Chappy ferry

CHAPPAQUIDDICK

LONG
POINT

Katama
Bay

KATAMA
POINT

Edgartown Bay Rd.

START

WASQUE RESERVATION

Atlantic Ocean

KATAMA BAY

THE COURSE

1. From the boat landing, head southwest into calm Mattakesett Bay. This section tends to be rather shallow, so don't get too close to shore unless you wish to stop and swim. Follow the barrier beach west.

    The closer you get to Chappaquiddick, the deeper the water, until you reach the western edge, where it becomes shallow. Wasque Reservation (chapter 20) lies at the western point. It offers hiking trails, restrooms, and beaches along the south and east coasts.

2. Proceed north for a good view of the homes along Chappaquiddick's shore.

3. Continue paddling through the lower harbor until you reach Caleb's Pond, an inlet off the east coast. Upon entering the pond, keep to the left, and then hug the shore to prevent going aground in this shallow section. Once you enter the main pond, the water becomes deeper. The calm water and isolation provides a striking contrast to the busy harbor.

    If you continue north after exploring the pond, you will enter Edgartown's inner harbor. The ferry shuttling back and forth between Chappaquiddick and Edgartown is named "On Time." The name refers to the short time period between ferry stops—since two ferries shuttle between the towns, one ferry is never more than a minute away from either side.

4. At the ferry dock, make a U-turn to head south down the Edgartown side of the bay.

    In the inner harbor old and elegant homes are perched by the water. As you progress south, you will have an excellent view of the huge mansions overlooking the bay.

    Just before you reach the boat landing, you'll see Katama Point, a spit of land jutting out into the water. A small property owned by the Martha's Vineyard Land Bank, the preserve features a short trail, small beach, and osprey (chapter 3).

CHAPTER THIRTY-FOUR

Eel Pond—Edgartown Outer Harbor

Action, accessibility, options! You may have to contend with boat traffic, which can be challenging, interesting, and lively in its own right, but paddling in Edgartown's outer harbor offers many other less congested options. A northeast route allows exploration of Eel Pond, nestled in Lighthouse Beach's protective peninsula. Its shallow waters draw shell fishermen and shorebirds seeking mollusks that inch along under the sand. You'll experience relaxed paddling in the pond and through the marsh but a bit more challenge as you head north into Nantucket Sound and then return south to weave around the boats in Edgartown Harbor. For additional paddling, you can continue south through Edgartown's inner harbor to Katama Bay (chapter 33) or head east to Chappaquiddick and Cape Poge Bay (chapter 37).

Lighthouse Beach, which extends 1 mile from Eel Pond to Edgartown Harbor, offers opportunities for swimming, picnicking, bird-watching, shelling, and sunbathing.

Directions: The boat launch is located off Braley's Lane in Edgartown. From the intersection of Main Street and Pease's Point Way, head north on Pease's Point Way, following the signs to the Chappaquiddick ferry. Remain on Pease's Point Way until it ends at Braley's Lane. Turn left. Take the third right (look for a white picket fence). Follow the road to the boat launch area. After you unload your boat, you can park on either side of the road.

Distance: The route described is approximately 6 miles (not including the optional explorations) but is easily shortened or lengthened.

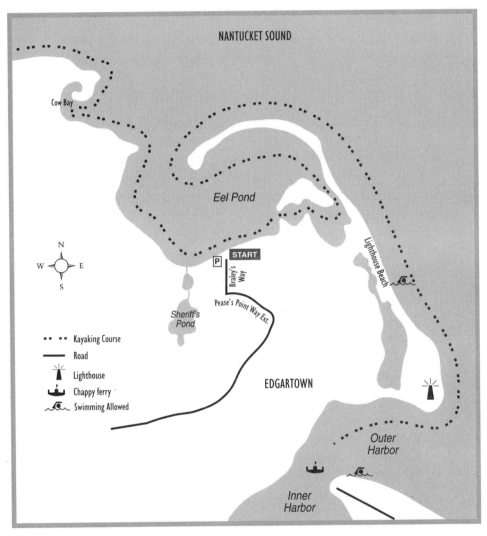

EEL POND AND EDGARTOWN OUTER HARBOR

Difficulty: Moderate. Because some paddling is on the ocean (albeit on the calm north side), winds and current may be strong. Because the area around Lighthouse Beach is very shallow, running aground is a real possibility. If you continue into Edgartown Harbor, be alert to boat traffic and the wakes that follow.

THE COURSE

1. From the boat launch, turn left in a northerly direction, following the shore of Eel Pond.

   The undeveloped land is Sheriff's Meadow Sanctuary, which has walking trails that overlook Eel Pond (chapter 16).

   Eel Pond ends at a marsh, a bird-watcher's delight. You may spot **American oystercatchers**, black-and-white birds that use their long, pointed red bills to pry open mollusks. Their competition may be small brown birds with skinny yellow legs and long pointed bills, named **lesser yellowlegs**.

2. Continuing past the marsh, paddle around the rocks and make a sharp left turn to head into Nantucket Sound. This route skirts Cow Bay and ends at the 3-mile-long John Sylvia State Beach on the north shore.

The view looking inland from Eel Pond.

3. To return, head back into Eel Pond, passing your starting point to wind your way in and out of the salt marsh that lies behind Lighthouse Beach.

After exploring the marsh, go around the peninsula (watch for the sandbars) and follow the beach south as it heads toward Edgartown Lighthouse and the harbor. You may be accompanied by **least terns**, small white birds with black caps that dive headfirst into the water for fish.

The Edgartown Lighthouse sits at the entrance to Edgartown Harbor. The lighthouse originally was built on a man-made island of granite blocks that was connected to the mainland by a wooden walkway. When the walkway eroded, a causeway was built to replace it. Natural forces created a replacement for the causeway when water currents formed a small barrier beach, now named Lighthouse Beach.

4. If you decide to continue your trip south toward Katama Bay, carefully cross between the two ferry boats that continuously shuttle cars, bikes, and pedestrians between Edgartown and Chappaquiddick.

If you wish to swim in deeper water, cross to the Chappaquiddick side of the harbor. A small beach owned by the Martha's Vineyard Land Bank lies just north of the On Time ferry dock. By following the long stretch of beach on Chappaquiddick's north shore, you'll eventually land in Cape Poge Bay.

CHAPTER THIRTY-FIVE

Edgartown Great Pond

At the end of a bumpy dirt road lies the public boat launch for Edgartown Great Pond, a wide body of water with one long cove and several shorter ones. These protected coves make Edgartown Great Pond a great place to paddle and a favorite of kayak rental companies. It can take most of a day to explore all the coves, or a couple of hours to visit one. Swimming is possible off the small beach at the launching area or in the ocean on the opposite side of the barrier beach.

Directions: From the intersection of Airport Road and the Edgartown–West Tisbury Road, travel east 2.5 miles on the Edgartown–West Tisbury Road to Meeting House Way. Turn right and proceed 1.3 miles down this unpaved and very rutted road. Turn right onto another dirt road, distinguished by a grassy island between two entrances. Follow this road for 0.8 mile to the public landing. Drop your boat off at the end of the road and park around the circle.

Size: The pond is 1.5 miles long and 0.5 mile wide. The distance from the open pond to the tip of the longest cove, Wintucket, is approximately 2 miles.

Difficulty: Moderate. Windy conditions from the southwest often prevail on the open pond, especially from 2:30 to 5:00 P.M., but the sheltered coves offer protection. The pond is quite shallow and the coves more so.

THE COURSE

1. Begin at the public landing on Meshacket Cove. If you prefer "get-away-from-it-all" paddling, head for the west side of the pond. At the southeast edge lies Job's Neck Cove, an undeveloped inlet bordered by marsh grass. Leaving the cove and proceeding north reveals a tiny pond

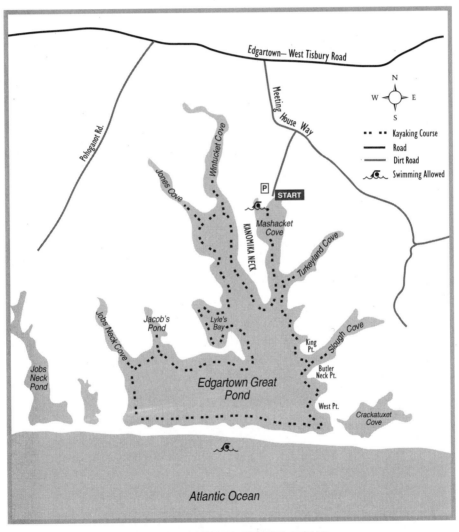

⬩ EDGARTOWN GREAT POND

tucked behind the grass. High tide may allow passage into the pond. Ahead lies Lyles Bay.

2. To visit my favorite spot, Jane's Cove, continue to follow the western shore.

    Paddling to the tip of the cove reveals a landscape inhabited only by wildlife. Tall trees and decayed tree trunks provide perfect habitats for a variety of shorebirds. The last time I was there, I saw an osprey nest in its original habitat—a dead tree trunk, not the telephone poles that serve as subsitute nesting platforms all over the island. A great blue heron flew away as I approached, leaving her brown youngster perched on a dead limb. The young heron was too busy looking around for its mother to notice me, so I was able to get close enough to practically touch it before it dropped into the water and paddled away. Allow about two hours to visit Job's Neck and Jane's Coves.

3. When returning to Meshacket Cove, head south toward the barrier beach. When you reach the open pond and are across from the beach, head north. Meshacket and the boat landing are directly across from the beach. The cove is distinguished by a gray shingled house at the midpoint of its northern tip.

    If you wish to explore the largest cove, Wintucket, allow two hours. Paddling from Meshacket to Slough and Turkeyland Coves on the east side takes approximately an hour and a half.

4. To see Wintucket Cove, proceed out of Meshacket Cove and turn right, passing Kanomika Neck on your right.

    Here you can forage for your lunch, as the southern tip of Kanomika Neck often is studded with clams. The wide cove branches into two smaller ones: Jane's Cove on the left and the longer Wintucket Cove on the right. If you paddle to the tip of Wintucket Cove, you'll come to a weir placed across the inlet to divert the water. While paddling in these narrow coves, stay in the middle to avoid the shallow coastline.

    Two small coves lie east of Mashacket Cove. The first, Turkeyland Cove, is less developed than Slough Cove, the first cove to be developed, and is lined with older cottages. The other coves have fewer houses because each of these newer homes sit on at least three acres of land.

5. When returning from the east side of the pond, remember that Turkeyland and Meshacket Coves form a V, with the boat launch on the left side of the V.

CHAPTER THIRTY-SIX

Poucha Pond

Poucha is a small, shallow, sheltered pond, perfect for inexperienced paddlers. One can paddle in the open pond or weave in and out of the salt marsh, a favorite nesting and feeding spot for a variety of shorebirds such as kingfishers, great blue herons, American oystercatchers, herring gulls, cormorants, and snowy egrets. Poucha Pond borders two conservation areas: Wasque Reservation and Poucha Pond Reservation. Wasque offers hiking trails, picnic benches, and the opportunity to jump the waves on the south coast or swim off the calmer eastern shore.

The Trustees of Reservations, which manages East Beach, offers naturalist-led canoe tours as well as canoe and kayak rentals from June to September. The rentals are for members only, but it is easy and relatively inexpensive to join.

More-intrepid and energetic paddlers can extend their trip by heading into Cape Poge Bay (chapter 37).

Directions: Take the ferry to Chappaquiddick. Travel 2.5 miles on Chappaquiddick Road. When the road bends sharply to the right, continue straight onto unpaved Dike Road. Follow Dike Road to the end at Dike Bridge and East Beach. Get there early, as parking is limited. Do not park along the road or you will be ticketed. If the lot is full, you can drop off your boat and park in the Mytoi parking lot, 0.2 mile back down Dike Road.

Fee: Round-trip fees for the Chappaquiddick ferry are $5 for car and driver; $1 for each additional passenger; $3 for cyclists.

Size: 1.4 miles long and 0.5 mile at its widest point

Difficulty: Easy. The only hazard is trying to paddle while slapping the greenhead flies in July and the mosquitoes in August—bring along bug repellent.

THE COURSE

1. Put in your boat to the right of Dike Bridge, named for a dike constructed in the mid-1800 to control the flow of water into Poucha Pond.

    In winter the dike was closed to keep the water fresh. In spring the gates of the dike were opened to allow herring and shad to swim into the pond and deposit their eggs in the protected waters.

2. Head south and stay to the right, following the marsh on the eastern shore. Turn right into the first inlet. You can paddle quite a way into this serene but smelly channel, passing the Marsh Trail through Mytoi on the right.

    As you paddle among the marsh grass, you may notice shorebirds surveying the water for their next meal. You can't miss the **American oystercatcher**, which sports a long, bright-orange bill and a dark brown upper body with a white belly. It's also easy to spot the **great blue heron**, mostly light gray with a yellow bill and a long neck and legs.

Great blue heron

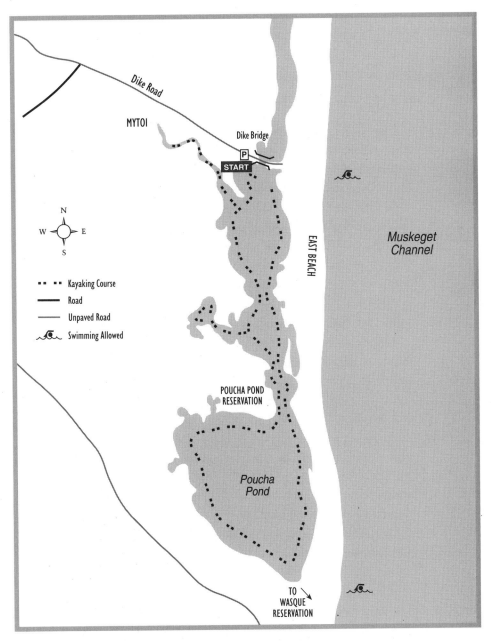

POUCHA POND

Two different types of grasses grow in the marsh. Growing next to the water is a stiff, spiky grass called **cordgrass**. The thinner-leaved grass that bends in the wind is called **salt-marsh hay**, used by early settlers to feed their sheep and cattle. As you paddle in and out of the marsh, you'll notice thousands of **Atlantic ribbed mussels** attached to the roots of the grass.

The course passes by a peninsula, a section of Poucha Pond Reservation. Because it is surrounded by marsh, it is difficult to pull your boat ashore to explore. In this section you may discover remnants of the vegetation planted by the Poucha Pond Meadow and Fishing Company, the Chappaquiddick landowners who built the dike. In the last hundred years new growth has replaced the old, but the vegetation continues to attract waterfowl, which was the purpose for the planting in the first place. Three varieties of herons feed in this area: the short green heron, the great blue heron, and the black-crowned night heron. You may also spot marsh hawks, egrets, and short-eared owls.

3. Follow the shore around until you reach the sandy southern tip.

A harbor was located here during pre-Colonial times, but by 1722 storms, winds, and tides had filled in the opening to the sea, and the water in the pond became increasingly fresh. By the 1800s, wild cranberries flourished at this end of the pond, and workers often harvested four barrels a day.

4. You can pull your boat ashore at the southeast corner to visit Wasque Reservation, a Trustees of Reservations property with hiking trails, toilets, and a magnificent beach with pounding surf (chapter 20). To head into the reservation, follow the path next to the fenced-in area (for the protection of terns and plovers) until you reach the water.

You probably will find fishermen at Wasque Point, the junction of the south and east coasts. Do not swim at the point because of dangerous rip tides. For big surf, turn right and swim along the south shore. For calmer water, turn left onto East Beach.

5. To return, follow the east coast north to Dike Bridge.

CHAPTER THIRTY-SEVEN

Cape Poge Bay

The most remote place to paddle is Cape Poge Bay, located on the northern tip of Chappaquiddick. Here sea gulls, and an occasional scallop fisherman, may be your only companions in this undeveloped "almost pond" (a narrow channel is the only opening to Nantucket Sound). There are plenty of terrific places to swim and sun, as the tour begins at East Beach and travels beside a 2.5-mile-long barrier beach in the Cape Poge Wildlife Refuge. Among the birds that nest and feed here are osprey, oystercatchers, piping plovers, and least and common terns.

Arrive early at East Beach. Parking is limited.

Directions: Take the ferry to Chappaquiddick (again, early is best; in the summer long lines are possible from 10:00 A.M. to 1:00 P.M. and on the return from 4:00 P.M. to 6:00 P.M.). Travel 2.5 miles on Chappaquiddick Road. When the road bends sharply to the right, continue straight onto unpaved Dike Road. Follow Dike Road to the end at Dike Bridge and East Beach. You can park only vertically on the west side of the lot. If the lot is full, go back down Dike Road 0.2 mile and park in the Mytoi lot.

Fee: Round-trip fees for the Chappaquiddick ferry are $5 for car and driver; $1 for each additional passenger; $3 for cyclists.

Size: 2.5 miles long; 1.2 miles wide. To cover the whole bay takes three to four hours.

Difficulty: Moderate. Because the bay is quite exposed, be prepared for wind and chop.

The Course

1. Launch your boat on the north (left) side of Dike Bridge. Hug the east shore as you paddle north through the lagoon toward Cape Poge Bay. Proceed toward the sandy beach straight ahead. Upon arrival at the beach you will see the opening into Cape Poge Bay. If you want to stop and swim in warm calm water, this protected spot just before the bay is a good choice.

2. Once in the bay, continue north, following the coastline. On the east side you'll see the 3-mile barrier beach of Cape Poge Wildlife Refuge. East of the refuge lies the Muskeget Channel in Nantucket Sound.

   In the shallow water you may spot a strange, dark form scuttling under the sand searching for soft-shelled clams. This large sea animal, known as a **horseshoe, or king, crab** is related to the scorpion and has been around since prehistoric times. Its long sharp tail at the end of its shell lowers for digging and rises to defend.

   In the middle of the pond where the water is deeper, you'll paddle over jungles of eel grass, home to fin- and shellfish which in turn attract shorebirds.

   Plan on paddling for an hour before arriving at a small peninsula, defined by an osprey pole, followed by a round inlet called Shear Pen Pond. The name refers to its use three hundred years ago, when sheep were herded here to be washed and then shorn of their wool.

   At the northeastern tip of the barrier beach sits Cape Poge Lighthouse, which has welcomed ships sailing into Edgartown Harbor since 1802. This lighthouse has replaced earlier ones, which were destroyed by winds or beach erosion.

   You'll notice that this section at the northernmost point of Cape Poge is more fertile than the barren eastern strip. Because the terrain here is so different from the rest of the barrier beach, some people believe it once was a separate island, now linked by the eventual build-

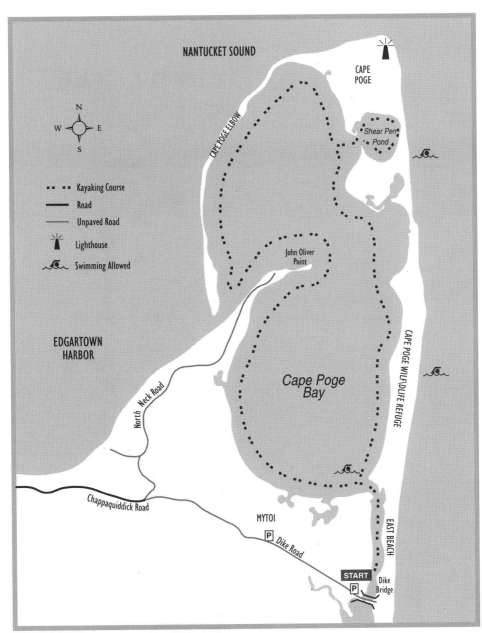

NANTUCKET SOUND

CAPE POGE

Shear Pen Pond

N
W   E
S

- - - - Kayaking Course
——— Road
——— Unpaved Road
Lighthouse
Swimming Allowed

CAPE POGE ELBOW

John Oliver Point

EDGARTOWN HARBOR

CAPE POGE WILDLIFE REFUGE

Cape Poge Bay

North Neck Road

Chappaquiddick Road

MYTOI

P Dike Road

EAST BEACH

START
P Dike Bridge

CAPE POGE BAY

up of sand caused by winds and ocean currents. Some historians believe this linkage could have occurred as early as the thirteenth century, while others are of the opinion that this area remained an island until the early 1700s.

3. Continue around the tip of the bay, now heading south, to paddle next to Cape Poge Elbow, a slender strip of land inhabited by herring and black-backed gulls.

   These gulls subsist mainly on shellfish. To break open the hard crustaceans, the gulls fly into the air with their victims in their beaks and then fling them onto hard areas. If you visit in June, the Elbow will be littered with gull eggs and the protective mothers will divebomb any intruder.

4. Cape Poge Elbow ends at Cape Poge Gut, a narrow opening with a swift current that leads to Edgartown Harbor and Nantucket Sound. At this point, head east to skirt North Neck and then pass by a more developed section.

5. Upon reaching the eastern side of Chappaquiddick, turn south to return via the lagoon to Dike Bridge.

CHAPTER THIRTY-EIGHT

Sengekontacket Pond

Sengekontacket, a Native American name meaning "at the bursting forth of the tidal stream," lies next to Joseph Sylvia State Beach. The pond makes the ride on Beach Road between Oak Bluffs and Edgartown one of the most picturesque on the island. This is not your "get-away-from-it-all" pond. Some sections are built up, but the lovely homes, scattered windsurfers, and occasional clammers should not interfere with your paddling pleasure.

Sengekontacket offers plenty of diversions: rest stops at two tiny deserted islands; strolling along the trails and viewing the waterfowl at Felix Neck Wildlife Sanctuary, Pecoy Point Preserve, and Caroline Tuthill Preserve; sneaking a closer look at the golfers teeing off at Farm Neck Golf Course; weaving your way through the inlet that leads to a salt marsh at the end of Majors Cove; and swimming in the pond or the ocean.

Directions: The public boat ramp is located on the south side of Beach Road, 1.8 miles from the Oak Bluffs terminal and 3.2 miles from the intersection with the Edgartown–Vineyard Haven Road in Edgartown. Look for Andy's Frozen Lemonade stand, which often sits in the parking area. You can park in the lot or along Beach Road.

Distance: 2.5 miles long and 0.5 mile wide. It takes three to four hours to paddle around the entire pond.

Difficulty: Easy to moderate, depending on the wind. If paddling in the summer with the wind out of the southwest, explore in the morning and early afternoon, as the wind increases later in the day.

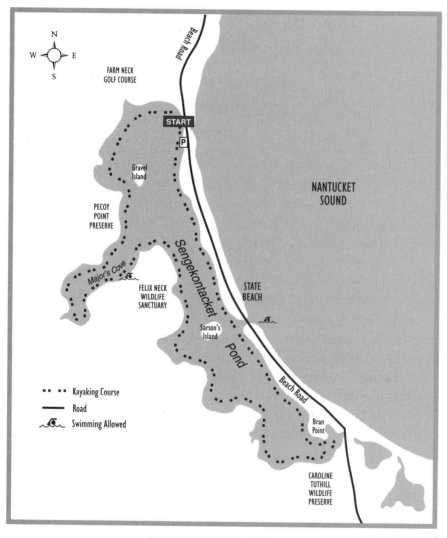

⟵ SENGEKONTACKET POND

THE COURSE

1. From the boat launching area, head right (north) to swing by Farm Neck, the most scenic and most popular golf course on the island.

    Luxurious homes border the links, among them one belonging to film director Spike Lee.

2. Circle around the north end of the island, passing tiny Gravel Island on the left and a development, also named Sengekontacket, on the right. The Martha's Vineyard Land Bank has recently used the 2 percent fee tacked onto real estate purchases to acquire Pecoy Point Preserve, ahead on the right. If you wish to explore the preserve, you can secure your boat at the boat slide.

3. A right turn into an inlet named Major's Cove affords a glimpse on the left of Felix Neck Wildlife Sanctuary, owned by the Massachusetts Audubon Society. If the tide is high, hug the right side of the cove and paddle through a narrow channel into a scenic salt marsh often frequented by mallards, geese, swans, great blue herons, and osprey.

4. Return from the cove to the pond by paddling on the right, or south, side to literally have a bird's-eye view of Felix Neck. Ahead on the right is a small sandy beach where you can pull up your boat if you wish to explore the property (see chapter 18).

5. Returning from Major's Cove to the open pond, bend right to follow the shoreline. The center of the pond around Sarson's Island, on your left, is quite shallow.

    Sarson's Island, owned by Felix Neck, is often covered with hundreds of black birds with outstretched wings, long necks, and hooked beaks, named **double-crested cormorants**. While searching for the pound of fish they consume each day, the cormorants skim the pond, their wings often catching water with each flap. Because their bodies don't produce enough oil to easily

Cormorant

shed water, as is the case with ducks, geese, and swans, cormorants stop frequently to open their wings and dry. See if you can catch one taking off; they are quite heavy and often first drop to the water before gaining height.

6. Bear right into the bay, passing another salt marsh, a favorite nesting and feeding place for waterfowl, that borders the east side of Felix Neck. Look for brightly colored **wood ducks** swimming amidst the grass.

Majors Cove, an inlet of Sengekontacket Pond .

7. As you continue toward the east end of the pond, you'll notice that the homes are more crowded and sit at the edge of the shore.

   The older homes on the Vineyard did not have the newer conservation codes that require dwellings be built at least 100 feet from the water.

   The wooded area at the northeastern tip is the **Caroline Tuthill Preserve**, a property owned by another conservation organization, Sheriff's Meadow. If you wish to stretch your legs and pick some blueberries while taking a pleasant 1.3-mile walk, pull up your boat at the clearing and refer to chapter 17.

8. Continue around the east end of the pond, past the tiny peninsula called Bran Point. You likely will spot adults and children armed with nets gathering crabs from Menada Creek.

The return skirts the southeast shore, where you can pull up your boat and stop for a swim, either in the shallow pond or across the road from State Beach. As you paddle the remaining 2 miles back to your starting point, you can watch cyclists, in-line skaters, and joggers providing visual entertainment on the Beach Road bike path, the most popular on the island.

CHAPTER THIRTY-NINE

Lagoon Pond

If you are looking for a central location to launch your boat or just want a boat to launch, Lagoon Pond is for you. Separated by a causeway and drawbridge from Vineyard Haven Harbor, this deep pond serves as refuge for boats during major storms. Small pleasure craft are moored in the pond and often line up behind the drawbridge—it opens frequently—to enter Vineyard Sound. You too have the choice of heading into the harbor, but don't bother waiting for the bridge to open—you can paddle under it. If you want to escape the powerboats, paddle into the cove on the western side of the lagoon or head down to the southern tip. Try to avoid weekends when boat traffic is the heaviest.

Half of Lagoon Pond is in the town of Tisbury; the other half is in Oak Bluffs. The tour follows the Tisbury shore and returns on the Oak Bluffs side.

Winds Up, located about 500 feet from the public boat launch, provides rentals (and lessons too). Other options include exploring the Ramble Trail Preserve, stopping at the state lobster hatchery for a tour, or swimming off a public beach at the pond.

Directions: The state boat launch is on Beach Road in Vineyard Haven, 0.6 mile east of the Steamship Authority terminal and 0.2 west of the drawbridge.

Distance: 2 miles long and 0.4 mile wide. Allow a couple of hours to tour the pond.

Difficulty: Easy to moderate. There usually is not much wind or current, but boats entering and exiting do create wakes.

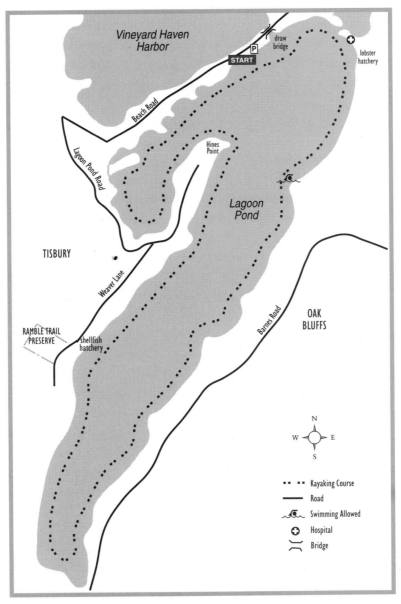

LAGOON POND

THE COURSE

1. From the launch site head west, following the northern shore. Windsurfers, kayakers, and sailors cluster around Winds Up, the store that rents and sells boats.

2. Continue into the cove, lined with businesses and boat yards but no boat traffic (too shallow). Circle around the peninsula called Hines Point. Be careful not to run aground in this shallow section.

   For more-tranquil paddling, head down the western, Tisbury side toward the southern tip of the pond.

   Once you are halfway down the coast and have entered a small bay, watch for rectangular containers in the water near the shore. These containers belong to the **Martha's Vineyard Shellfish Hatchery** and are used to propagate shellfish. Lagoon Pond is seeded for scallops, and you may spot fishermen digging for the succulent mollusks. In front of the hatchery rest a number of "boxes" used for scallop propagation.

   South of the shellfish hatchery lies the **Ramble Trail Preserve**, a small property owned by the Martha's Vineyard Land Bank. To identify the property, look for a number of boats lying on the beach. Behind the boats, stairs lead to the trails. You can hike to the top of the bluff for an overview of Lagoon Pond and stroll along the Ramble Trail, one of the first paths constructed on the island for recreational walking.

   Shorebirds frequent this more remote section. Black **cormorants** dry their wings on rafts and docks, colorful **mallards** paddle by, and **herring gulls** search for supper.

3. After circling around the tip and heading north (often helped by a tail-wind), you leave the Tisbury side of the pond and enter Oak Bluffs.

   About halfway up you'll notice a sandy strip, often inhabited by sun-bathers and swimmers. The southern half belongs to landowners, but the northern section is public. Feel free to stop and swim.

   Farther up the coast, a silo marks the site of the **state lobster hatchery**. Here researchers study the living habits of lobsters. The Martha's Vineyard Hospital sits next to the hatchery.

4. If you wish to enter Vineyard Haven Harbor, paddle under the draw-bridge. Watch for boats entering and exiting.

5. To return to the boat launch, pass the bridge and continue paddling west for a few more minutes.

CHAPTER FORTY

Lake Tashmoo

For a preview of coming attractions, stop at the Lake Tashmoo Overlook on State Road to watch boats motoring in and out of Vineyard Sound. From this picture-postcard setting, it's a five-minute drive to this small, picturesque lake. Lake Tashmoo is a good choice if you want a short excursion and/or a swim in Vineyard Sound. My favorite areas are the quiet coves on the southern and northwestern tips.

Check the tide schedule, as the northeast side of the lake can become quite shallow during low tide.

Directions: From State Road in Tisbury, go north on West Spring Street (just east of the Tashmoo Overlook). Bear left at the stop sign. Take the second left onto Pine Street. At the next stop sign, turn left onto Lake Street. Follow Lake until it ends at the Tisbury Town Landing. You are allowed to park for four hours in the lot on the south side of the road.

Size: 1.4 miles long; 0.6 mile at its widest point. It takes about ninety minutes to circumnavigate the lake.

Difficulty: Easy. Because Tashmoo is small and sheltered, wind and chop seldom present a problem. But you will have to contend with boat traffic and current in the channel.

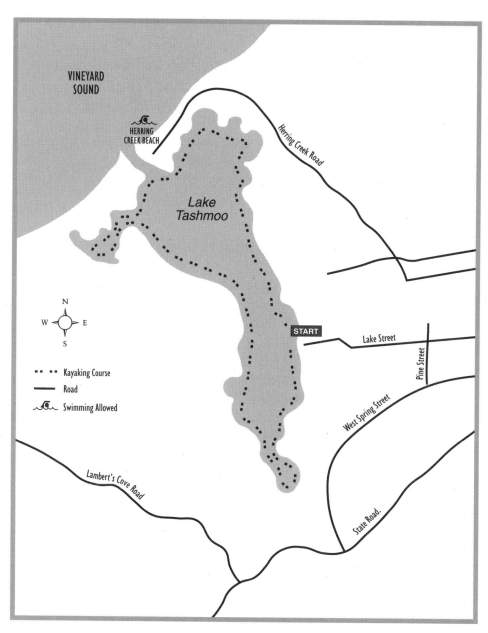

VINEYARD
SOUND

HERRING
CREEK BEACH

Herring Creek Road

Lake
Tashmoo

N
W E
S

START

Lake Street

Pine Street

- - - Kayaking Course

—— Road

Swimming Allowed

West Spring Street

Lambert's Cove Road

State Road.

LAKE TASHMOO

THE COURSE

1. From the dock, head north and paddle around the sail, fishing, and motor boats moored in this small harbor. Follow the shoreline and try to stay away from the channel, which runs down the middle of the lake, where fighting the current and dodging boat traffic can alter your course.

2. Follow the coast as it bends east. This section can be quite shallow, so you may get exercise from pulling and pushing your boat rather than paddling. Herring Creek Beach is located on the northeast side of the lake. Here you can swim at the lifeguard-supervised beach on the sound, lie in the sun, or wade in the lake.

3. To cross to the west side of the lake, carefully traverse the channel and watch for boats entering from Vineyard Sound.

    Perched on the northwest corner of the outlet to the ocean sits an imposing residence named Chip Chop, former home of actress Katherine Cornell and now owned by television newswoman Diane Sawyer and director Mike Nichols.

4. Head west into the calm cove, and then go all the way down to the southern tip to explore the less developed section of the lake. Here the only traffic you have to contend with is from ducks and geese paddling about.

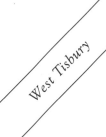

CHAPTER FORTY-ONE

Tisbury Great Pond

Tisbury Great Pond resembles a hand with five fingers, each finger a cove and the thumb Black Point Pond. You can easily spend a day exploring these narrow, picturesque coves and pristine Black Point Pond.

The water level in Tisbury Great Pond fluctuates greatly, depending on when the pond has been opened to the sea. Workers cut a breach through the barrier beach when the pond reaches a certain height, so the resident oysters will have the salt water they need to breed. Do wear foot covering to protect against the oyster's sharp shells and pincers from the blue-claw crab. If you bring along a bucket and net, you can attempt to catch the elusive crabs that emerge in late afternoon.

You can stop to picnic, hike, and swim at Sepiessa Point Reservation or Long Point Reservation.

Directions: The boat launch site is at Sepiessa Point Reservation. To reach the reservation, proceed 3 miles west of the entrance to the Martha's Vineyard Airport on the Edgartown–West Tisbury Road. Turn left onto New Lane. Follow New Lane for 1.2 miles. Turn right onto Clam Point Way, a dirt road that leads to the reservation. Continue on the road about 500 feet past the first parking area to the second parking lot. It's a short walk to haul your boat into Tiah's Cove. If you prefer to spend more time driving than paddling, proceed 1 mile to the end of the dirt road and unload your boat farther up the cove.

Size: The pond itself is about 1 mile long and a 0.5 mile wide. The coves range from 0.5 to 2 miles long. You could easily spend a day exploring the pond, or an hour or two in one of the coves.

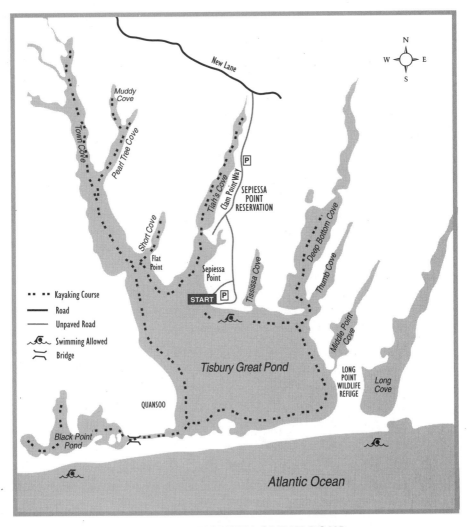

TISBURY GREAT POND

Difficulty: Moderate. On windy days or after 2:30 P.M., when the wind increases, you may have difficulty paddling southwest into the wind on the open pond. The sheltered coves usually present no problem.

THE COURSE

1. Paddle out Tiah's Cove to Tisbury Great Pond. Head right to explore the longest finger, Town Cove. Allow an hour and a half for a leisurely investigation of this undeveloped section, consisting mainly of farmland. The first inlet on the right is Short Cove, followed by Pear Tree Cove, which branches into Muddy Cove.

2. From Town Cove, head south toward the barrier beach. The narrow channel to Black Point Pond remains hidden until you reach the barrier beach.

    To visit this tranquil pond, turn right down the channel. Unless the water level is low, you should have no trouble paddling between the marsh grass. Make sure you duck your head when passing under the bridge to the pond. It's worth the effort to navigate the channel, as you are likely to be the only nonwaterfowl inhabitant of this undeveloped spot. You can explore its coves, stop for a swim, and admire the **great blue herons** that frequent the pond.

3. From Black Point Pond, you can return by following the barrier beach east toward Long Point Wildlife Refuge. If the water level in Tisbury Great Pond appears low, a breach has recently been cut. Look toward the west side of the barrier beach for a narrow channel running out to the sea (often filled with children riding the current).

4. Continue past the barrier beach, following the coast as it turns north.

    Long Point Reservation, a Trustees of Reservations property described in chapter 25, lies on your right. If you wish to stop for a swim or hike its trails, pull your boat onto the beach. Stairs ascend from the shore to a path. If you go right, you'll discover a glorious beach. A left turn leads to hiking trails.

5. Proceeding around the pond, the next cove, Middle Point Cove, has not actually reached cove status. However, it's just a matter of time before the land separating the "almost cove" from the pond will be washed away and it really will become a cove.

Tisbury Great Pond.

6. Next are the "two-for-the-price-of-one" coves. As you head into Thumb Cove, you'll discover that it forks, revealing Deep Bottom Cove as well. Allow an hour to explore these two coves.

7. The last cove is Tississa Cove, which flanks the east side of Sepiessa Point Reservation (chapter 26). If you wish to end your trip with a swim or a hike through the reservation, pass Tississa Cove and pull your boat up onto the sand. If you have parked near the boat launch at Tiah's Cove, you have the option of following the Red Trail 1 mile through the reservation to your car and then driving back to pick up your boat.

8. If you are returning on the open pond from the barrier beach or Black Point Pond, finding Tiah's Cove can be tricky. My locator points are the red barn on the west side of Tississa Cove, the beach at Sepiessa Point, and the osprey pole in Sepiessa next to the boat launch at the southern end of Tiah's Cove.

CHAPTER FORTY-TWO

Chilmark Pond

Chilmark Pond, the smallest body of water in this guide, compensates for its small size by offering variety, tranquillity, beauty, and many species of shorebirds. One of several narrow coves in Chilmark Lower Pond leads to Doctors Creek, which snakes its way through dense marsh grass to Chilmark Upper Pond, where yet another cove awaits exploration. Swimming is nearby at a Land Bank–owned section of spectacular Hancock Beach.

Public access to Chilmark Pond was denied until 1993, when the Martha's Vineyard Land Bank purchased 8.3 acres of land that adjoined the pond and a portion of private beach. The Land Bank constructed an access road, small parking lot, and boat launching area.

Directions: From the intersection of the Edgartown–West Tisbury Road and South Road in the town of West Tisbury, head west 3.2 miles. It's easy to miss the tiny Land Bank sign on the crest of the hill on the left side. Turn left and follow the road to the small parking lot. Get there early to guarantee a spot. (There is room for only ten cars.)

Distance: 2 miles long and 0.25 mile wide. Allow a couple of hours to explore both the upper and lower ponds.

Difficulty: Easy. Relaxed paddling, unless there is a strong southwest wind. Doctors Creek requires perseverance and some skillful paddling.

THE COURSE

The depth of this freshwater pond varies, depending on when an opening has been cut in the barrier beach. If you visit in May or early June, right after the opening of the pond to the ocean, you will find a much shallower pond than in late summer.

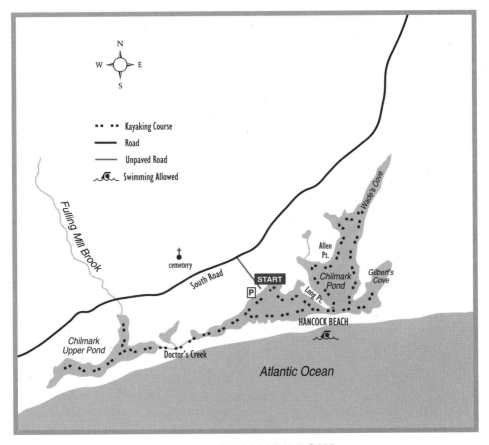

CHILMARK POND

1. After launching your boat, head left into a small cove. Proceed to a longer narrower inlet, Wade's Cove, at the northeast tip of the pond.

   Shorebirds often congregate around the marsh grass. The last time I visited, I spotted a great blue heron, swans, double-crested cormorants, mottled ducks, Canada geese, herring gulls, and common terns.

2. Proceed up the east side of the pond to head into Gilbert's Cove. This section tends to be shallow, so you may not get too far. If you are interested in sunning and swimming at the Land Bank beach, head west about 0.25 mile. Look for two orange flags that mark the Land Bank boundaries. A boardwalk and stairs lead from the pond to the beach.

3. From the beach continue west to Doctor's Creek, the narrow, overgrown connector to Chilmark Upper Pond.

   If you enter, be advised that at times you will be convinced that the phragmites have taken over and that there is no outlet to the next pond. But persevere and you will emerge. The return will be much easier because the current will push you along. Your paddling companions will be blue-claw crabs that skitter along the creek floor.

4. Now in Upper Pond, look to the west at the colorful cliffs of Lucy Vincent Beach. Paddle north to explore Warren Tilton Cove, where the Fulling Mill Brook ends. Loop around the pond and head back along the south shore to return through Doctor's Creek to Lower Pond.

CHAPTER FORTY-THREE

Menemsha Pond
Nashaquitsa Pond
Stonewall Pond

At the narrow western end of Martha's Vineyard, you can almost paddle from the Atlantic Ocean to Vineyard Sound. The course begins at Stonewall Pond on the south shore and runs under South Road to Nashaquitsa Pond, which flows into Menemsha Pond, located on the north side of the island. You can stop to swim at the sandy beach on the northeast side of Menemsha Pond on your way to Menemsha Basin, which opens into Vineyard Sound.

Each of these bodies of water has its own character: Stonewall Pond is small, sheltered, and often filled with shorebirds. Nashaquitsa Pond appears as a small, protected harbor with several long coves. Menemsha Pond is quite the opposite—open, often windy, the perfect location for its weekly regattas.

Directions: The boat launch for Nashaquitsa Pond is located on South Road, 1.3 miles west of Beetlebung Corner (the intersection of South, Middle and Menemsha Cross Roads in Chilmark Center). The small parking area is on the right side of the road, just past a small bridge. If you get to the Nashaquitsa Pond Overlook, you've gone too far.

Distance: 1 mile wide, 2 miles long. Each pond takes about an hour to paddle around, but if you are making the coast-to-coast trip, allow three to four hours.

Difficulty: Stonewall and Nashaquitsa Ponds are protected and usually calm. Windy conditions often exist on Menemsha Pond.

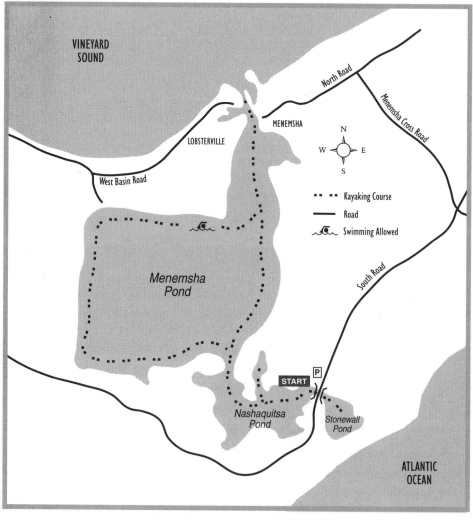

MENEMSHA , NASHAQUITSA, & STONEWALL PONDS

THE COURSE

1. From the boat launch at Nashaquitsa (known locally as Quitsa) Pond, turn right to paddle under the bridge to Stonewall Pond.

Canada geese and **mallards** often swim around the tiny pond. If you proceed straight across the pond, you'll find the path to Stonewall Beach. If you follow the path you'll discover how the pond and beach got their names.

2. Returning to Quitsa Pond, stay to the right if you are interested in exploring quiet coves, with nothing but dragonflies for company. The pond has several other coves to explore.

As you head from one cove to the next, you pass a large boulder resting in the middle of the pond, a favorite spot for **cormorants** to dry their wings.

3. Continue straight to head into Menemsha Pond. Be prepared for some chop and wind. It's best to visit during the week so you won't have to dodge sailboats. If you want to stop to sunbathe and swim, paddle to the sandy beach on the northeast side of the pond. Farther west along the beach, the water is too shallow for swimming.

Here you are likely to spot **least terns** swooping down to the water in their continual search for fish.

4. If you stay to the right of Menemsha Pond, you'll enter Menemsha Basin, a busy passageway for boats entering and exiting from Vineyard Sound.

The bike ferry shuttles bikes and their owners across the basin to Lobsterville. One hundred years ago, the now deserted Lobsterville was the premier fishing village on the island. It fell into disuse after the basin was dredged and Menemsha Harbor was created.

5. To return, you can skirt the perimeter of Menemsha Pond or head straight back. To find the launching ramp, keep your eyes out for the little bridge.

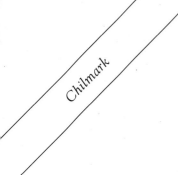

CHAPTER FORTY-FOUR

Squibnocket Pond

Sand dunes, rocky outcroppings, and small forested islands contribute to the rarefied experience of paddling around Squibnocket Pond, one of the least developed and most beautiful bodies of water on Martha's Vineyard. Located on the west end of the island, the parking lot for Squibnocket is easy to find. Unfortunately, visitors who are not residents of Aquinnah or Chilmark can not park there until after 5:00 P.M. during July and August. Parking is permitted in the spring and after Labor Day.

Directions: From Beetlebung Corner in Chilmark Center, travel west 2.1 miles. Turn left onto Squibnocket Road (no street sign), the first paved road on the left. Proceed to the parking lot at the end of the road.

Size: 1.8 miles wide, 1.2 miles long. Allow two hours to circle the pond.

Difficulty: Moderate. Much of the pond is open, so wind and chop are the norm.

THE COURSE

1. The exploration begins in a marshy inlet. You will have to navigate over tall grass, as this section is slowly reverting to swamp. Once out of

the inlet, you can head left and visit a salt marsh with calm waters and a variety of shorebirds.

2. To reach the open pond, continue straight. I suggest bearing right of the island and following the shore, but not too closely, due to rocky outcroppings. As you proceed north and then west, you'll find the pond slowly revealing itself. You'll think you have reached the farthest point, and suddenly you'll see another bay.

The large, two-story gray-shingled home with several additions spread over many acres belonged to Jacqueline Kennedy Onassis.

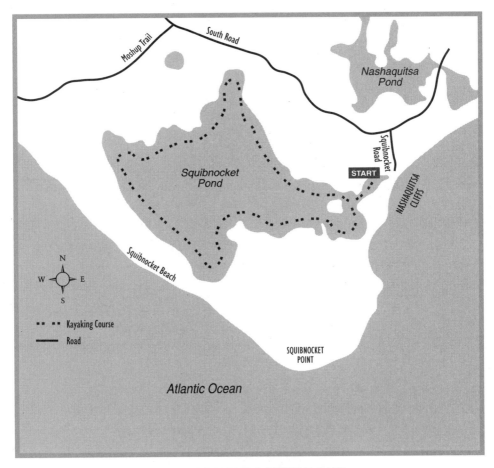

SQUIBNOCKET POND

Kayakers on an inlet of Squibnocket Pond.

3. When you paddle toward the sand dunes on the west side of the pond, you will hear the sound of the surf pounding against the shore of an exquisite beach that, sadly, is restricted to residents.

    Another sound may be the loud *whr-r-r* of swans taking off if you get too close. During my last visit I witnessed a convention of swans slowly paddling across the pond and hundreds of cormorants sunning themselves on the rocks.

4. To find your way back to the inlet, look for the small island and then paddle past it in a northwesterly direction.

APPENDIX

EMERGENCY

Ambulance, Fire, Police: 911.

Martha's Vineyard Hospital, Linton Lane, Oak Bluffs: 508-693-0410.

BICYCLE SHOPS

VINEYARD HAVEN

Cycleworks, 351 State Road, 693-6966. Rentals, sales, repairs.

Martha's Bicycle Rental, 4 Lagoon Pond Road, 693-0782. Rentals.

Martha's Vineyard Strictly Bikes, 24 Union Street, 693-0782.
Rentals, sales, repairs.

OAK BLUFFS

Bike Zone, 27 Lake Avenue, 693-9311. Sales, repairs

DeBettencourt's Bike Shop Inc., Circuit Avenue, 693-0011. Rentals.

Harbor Bike & Moped, Circuit Avenue Extension, 693-8852. Rentals.

Kings Rentals Inc., Circuit Avenue, 693-2613. Rentals.

Ride On Mopeds & Bikes, Lake Avenue, 693-2076. Rentals, sales, repairs.

Sun & Fun, 26 Lake Avenue, 693-5457. Rentals.

Two Wheel Traveler Moped & Bike Rentals, 23 Lake Avenue, 693-9147.

EDGARTOWN

Cutler, R. W., 1 Main Street, 627-4052. Rentals.

Edgartown Bicycles, 190 Upper Main Street, 627-9008. Rentals, sales, repairs.

Triangle Bike Shop, 241 Vineyard Haven Road, 627-7099. Rentals.

WEST TISBURY

West Tisbury Bike Shop, behind Alley's at 1041 State Road, 693-5495. Rentals, repairs.

Wheel Happy, 8 South Water Street, 627-5928. Rentals.

KAYAK RENTAL

TISBURY

Wind's Up, 199 Beach Road, 693-4252. Sales, rentals.

OAK BLUFFS

Bike Zone, 27 Lake Avenue, 696-9311. Rental, delivery.

EDGARTOWN

Gold Coast Parasail and Kayak Corp., Edgartown Harbor, 693-3330.
Rental, delivery.

Kasoon Kayak Company, 627-2553. Rental, delivery.

WEST TISBURY

Martha's Vineyard Kayak Co., 510 State Road, 693-0895. Rental, delivery.

CHILMARK

Menemsha Blues Oar and Paddle, 2 Basin Road, 645-3800.
Rentals, delivery.

PHARMACIES

VINEYARD HAVEN

Leslie's Drug Store, Main Street, 693-1010.

Medicine Shoppe Pharmacy, 40 Beach Road, 693-7979.

EDGARTOWN

Triangle Pharmacy, 245 Vineyard Haven Road, 627-5107.

WEST TISBURY

Conroy Apothecary, State Road, 693-7070.

HARDWARE STORES

VINEYARD HAVEN

Hinckley's Ace Hardware Store, Beach Road, 693-0075.
Shirley's True Value Hardware, 374 State Road, 693-3070.
Vineyard Home Center, 426 State Road, 693-3227.

OAK BLUFFS

Phillips Hardware, 30 Circuit Avenue, 693-0377.

EDGARTOWN

Edgartown Hardware Inc., Main Street, 627-4338.
Granite Five & Ten Ace Hardware, 242 Vineyard Haven Road,
627-3232.

WEST TISBURY

Alley's General Store, State Road, 693-0088.

MARKETS

VINEYARD HAVEN

A & P Food Store, Water Street, 693-9845.
Cronig's Market, State Road, 693-4457.
Cumberland Farms, Five Corners, 693-9869.
Food 'N' Go, 40 Beach Road, 693-9300.
Vineyard Grocery Outlet, 100 State Road, 693-0470.
Woodland Variety Store, State Road, 693-6795.

OAK BLUFFS

Our Market, East Chop Drive, 693-3000.
Reliable Self-Service Market, Circuit Avenue, 693-1102.
Tony's Market, Duke's County Avenue, 693-4799.

EDGARTOWN

A & P Food Store, Upper Main Street, 627-9522.
Katama General Store, 170 Katama Road, 627-5071.
Village Rotisserie, 199 Upper Main Street, 627-7784.
Your Market, Great Harbor Triangle, 627-4000.

WEST TISBURY

Alley's General Store, State Road, 693-0088.
Up Island Cronig's Market, State Road, 693-2234.

CHILMARK

Chilmark Store, State Road, 645-3739.
Menemsha Market, North Road, 645-3501.

SERVICE STATIONS

VINEYARD HAVEN

Tisbury Texaco, 9 Beach Road, 696-7275.

OAK BLUFFS

Cottage City Texaco, Lake Avenue, 690-0922.
DeBettencourt & Sons, New York Avenue, 693-0751.

EDGARTOWN

Airport Service Station, 3 North Line Road, 693-5559.
Edgartown Mobil, 199 Upper Main Street, 627-4715.

WEST TISBURY

Up-Island Automotive, State Road, 693-5166.

MENEMSHA

Menemsha Texaco Service Inc., Basin Road, 645-2641.

AUTOMOBILE PARKING AREAS FOR CYCLISTS

VINEYARD HAVEN

Tisbury School, between Spring and William Streets (when school is out of session).

OAK BLUFFS

Martha's Vineyard Regional High School, Edgartown–Vineyard Haven Road (when school is out of session).

EDGARTOWN

Bike path entrance to the State Forest: two parking areas on the west side of Barnes Road, 0.5 mile and 1.3 miles south of the Edgartown–Vineyard Haven Road intersection.

Edgartown–West Tisbury Road: across from Pohoganot Road, 1.6 miles east of Airport Road.

State Forest: east side of Barnes Road, 0.8 mile south of the intersection with the Edgartown–Vineyard Haven Road.

Trolley shuttle lots: Dark Woods Road, off the Edgartown–Vineyard haven Road, east of the triangle.

Robinson Road: between Pease's Point Way and the Edgartown–West Tisbury Road.

WEST TISBURY

Bike path entrances to the State Forest: Old County Road, 1 mile south of the State Road intersection.

Edgartown–West Tisbury Road, 1.6 miles west of the airport entrance road and across from Pond Road.

ABOUT THE AUTHOR

Lee Sinai, a Massachusetts resident, is also the author of *Exploring in and around Boston on Bike and Foot*, 2d edition. When Lee is not writing or creating maps, she is biking, hiking, in-line skating, skiing, or playing tennis.

Before becoming a writer, Lee's other careers included college administrator, director of tours and guides for a destination management company, tennis professional, teacher, wife, and mother. She received her undergraduate degree from the University of Michigan and a master's degree from Northwestern University.

About the AMC

A Tradition of Responsible Outdoor Recreation

Since 1876, the Appalachian Mountain Club has helped people experience the majesty and solitude of the Northeast outdoors. Our mission is to promote the protection, enjoyment, and wise use of the mountains, rivers, and trails of the Northeast. To that end, we offer workshops and guided trips, maintain outdoor facilities and hiking trails, and organize volunteer and conservation efforts. A nonprofit, a percentage of all our revenue goes toward our mission.

Over 80,000 members belong to one of 11 local AMC chapters in New Hampshire, Massachusetts, Connecticut, Maine, Rhode Island, New York, New Jersey and Washington, DC. All AMC programs and facilities are open to the public.

AMC Programs

Outdoor Adventures

Each year the AMC offers over 100 workshops on hiking, canoeing, cross-country skiing, biking, rock climbing and other outdoor activities. In addition to workshops, the AMC offers guided trips for hikers, canoers, and skiers.

Volunteering

AMC volunteers maintain over 1,400 miles of hiking trails in the Northeast, perform search and rescue operations in the White Mountains, clean up rivers, monitor water quality, and negotiate access to wilderness areas with private landowners.

Facilities

Mountain Huts

The AMC maintains eight huts in the White Mountains of New Hampshire. Staffed by AMC crews, these huts offer hikers a place to eat and sleep during their overnight hikes. Full service huts offer hikers hot meals, warm beds, and mountain hospitality, while self-service huts provide hikers with bunk beds.

Lodging and Visitor Services

In addition to its mountain huts, the AMC offers unique lodging and visitor services throughout the Northeast. Pinkham Notch Visitors Center offers lodging at the base of Mount Washington and offers hikers updated information on trail and weather conditions. Bascom Lodge sits atop Mt. Greylock in Massachusetts, Echo Lake Camp is on Mount Desert Island in ME, while the Mohican Outdoor Center is located in the Delaware Water Gap of western New Jersey.

Conservation Leadership

Outdoor recreation depends upon a commitment to protecting the land and keeping trails, rivers, and mountains accessible. The AMC has been at the forefront of the conservation movement since 1876. In 1911 the AMC fought to create the White Mountain National Forest. More recently, we have been active in protecting the Appalachian Trail corridor, securing access to trails and rivers, and protecting the Northeast Forest.

AMC Books and Maps — Since 1907

The Appalachian Mountain Club published its first trail guide in 1907. Today we offer an extensive line of trail guides, maps, and books on outdoor skills and conservation. We also publish *Appalachia*, the country's oldest mountaineering and conservation journal AMC books are written by experts who have spent years living among the rivers, hills, and mountains of the Northeast. Our books are backed by the expertise of the Appalachian Mountain Club and are intended to further our mission of promoting responsible outdoor recreation. Profits from AMC books support the AMC mission.

ALPHABETICAL LISTING OF AREAS

BY ACTIVITY

BIKING: ON-ROAD AND OFF-ROAD

KAYAKING

WALKING AND HIKING

INDEX

Numbers in boldface indicate an illustrated reference.

OTHER TITLES AVAILABLE FRON

APPALACHIAN MOUNTAIN CLUB BOOKS

TRAIL GUIDES

AMC White Mountain Guide
AMC Hiking Guide to Mount Washington and the Presidential Range
AMC Massachusetts and Rhode Island Trail Guide
AMC Maine Mountain Guide
AMC Southern New Hampshire Trail Guide
North Carolina Hiking Trails
West Virginia Hiking Trails
High Huts of the White Mountains

MULTI-RECREATIONAL GUIDES

Discover Acadia National Park
Exploring in and around Boston on Bike and Foot
Exploring the Hidden Charles

NATURE WALK GUIDES

Nature Walks in and around New York City
Nature Walks in Central and Western Massachusetts
Nature Walks in Eastern Massachusetts
Nature Walks near Philadelphia
Nature Walks in Southern New Hampshire
Nature Walks in Southern Maine
Nature Walks in Southern Vermont
Nature Walks in Northern Vermont
Nature Hikes in the White Mountains
More Nature Walks in Eastern Massachusetts

NATURE GUIDES

At Timberline
North Woods
AMC Field Guide to the New England Alpine Summits

PADDLESPORTS

Sea Kayaking Coastal Massachusetts
Sea Kayaking along the New England Coast
Sea Kayaking along the Mid-Atlantic Coast

AMC River Guide: Maine
AMC River Guide: Massachusetts/Connecticut/ Rhode Island
AMC River Guide: New Hampshire/Vermont

Quiet Water Canoe Guide: Maine
Quiet Water Canoe Guide: Massachusetts/ Connecticut/Rhode Island
Quiet Water Canoe Guide: New York
Quiet Water Canoe Guide: New Hampshire/Vermont

OUTDOOR SKILLS

Watercolor Painting on the Trail
The Complete Guide to Trail Building and Maintenance
AMC Guide to Freshwater Fishing in New England

FAMILY

Seashells in My Pocket